AN ORDINARY MAN IN EXTRAORDINARY TIMES

1st Edition

Published in 2021 by

Woodfield Publishing Ltd
Bognor Regis PO21 5EL England
www.woodfieldpublishing.co.uk

Cataloguing in Publication Data is available from the British Library

ISBN 978-1-84683-195-9

Printed and bound in England

Typesetting & page design: Nic Pastorius
Cover design: Klaus Schaffer

Source document:
An Ordinary Man in Exraordinary Times - Shipperbottom (final).ppp

An Ordinary Man in Extraordinary Times

The nautical adventures of an RAF High Speed Launch (HSL) Wireless Op/Signaller in the UK and Far East during World War II

PERCY SHIPPERBOTTOM

EDITED BY DAVID SHIPPERBOTTOM

woodfieldpublishing.co.uk
Woodfield Publishing Ltd
independent book publishers

Woodfield Publishing Ltd
West Sussex ~ England

Interesting & informative books on a wide variety of subjects

For full details about all our books, visit our website
www.woodfieldpublishing.co.uk

This book contains the reminiscences of a gamekeeper's grandson from Bolton, who joined the Royal Air Force as a 24-year-old volunteer in 1939 and went on to serve in the Air Sea Rescue service as a wireless operator and signaller on High Speed Launches patrolling in the English Channel during the Battle of Britain and later in the tropical waters of the Arakan Coast of Burma and the Bay of Bengal.

The job of the HSL crews was to rescue stranded airmen whose aircraft had ditched into the sea, often in extremely hazardous conditions and in this capacity these unsung heroes were responsible for saving many lives.

The Author, just after joining the RAF, 1939.

Contents

Grandad & Grandma, circa 1920s.

Introduction

OUR DAD WAS GREATLY INFLUENCED by his granddad, who raised, guided and mentored him, so this story begins with Dad's forefathers and in order to provide some background as to the attitudes and outlook on life for working-class mining families in the North West from the mid-1800s to the start of World War II.

I hope you find this story as interesting and enjoyable as much as I have had in preparing Dad's notes. In doing this I have discovered an insight into my forefathers which I feel privileged to see and the details of which I am sure would have been lost in time had Dad not decided to put him memories down in print. With the aid of the Internet and Google I have been able to provide historical backgrounds to some of the events in his life. I have written the story as though my Dad was narrating it and although I have prepared, edited and processed the text, they are my Dad's own words.

After his retirement he spent many hours at an old typewriter, patiently recalling his memories. I choose the word 'memories' carefully because these are not memoirs but simply an account of the first half of his life and military service. The story is told as my Dad relating it, so references to 'Grandad', etc are to *his* grandfather (i.e. my great-grandfather).

Dad continued to write as much as he could until arthritis in his hands (the result of over 25 years gripping the steering wheel of an HGV before power steering was the norm) and the slow onset of dementia, reduced his enthusiasm. Dad passed away quietly in a nursing home, aged 89. He did not remember the last few years after Mum died of a stroke some four years prior to his death. Unfortunately, neither of them lived to see this finished product. A pity really, he would have enjoyed seeing it finished, as Mum would.

David Shipperbottom, February 2021.

Bradshaw Hall.

Gamekeeper's cottage, Jumbles.

~ CHAPTER 1 ~

Family Background ~ 1835-1914

IN THE MID-1800S INDUSTRY IN Lancashire was booming. The damp climate and soft water favoured the cotton industry, cotton spinning and weaving being the main industry around Bolton. This in turn produced a thriving bleaching and dyeing industry to process the cloth produced in the vast number of 'dark satanic mills'.

The 'bleach works' were usually situated away from town and industrial centres, in the valleys where a large supply of clean water was available; a few small ones still survive today. This industry was powered by the proximity of a large number of lucrative coal seams, creating an equally large mining community.

All these industries were labour intensive and each cotton mill, bleach works and coal pit employed hundreds, if not thousands, of manual workers, most on a barely sustainable wage. Most of the mills were powered by steam and this needed a good supply of coal. The local landowners became coal mine owners and soon became rich and greedy and started to demand more output from the miners for less money. This led to industrial unrest and widespread strikes until the Lancashire coalfields practically ground to a halt. Strikes in the first quarter of the 19th century generally failed to improve pay and conditions and in 1830 miners formed the Friendly Society of Coal Mining, with its headquarters in Bolton.

To break the strikes the coal mine owners collaborated in a recruitment drive in Cornwall and recruited tin miners, who were being paid even less than the Lancashire coal miners. This understandably angered the Lancashire coal miners, who took action, and many fights broke out. The Cornish miners were easily recognisable, as they wore black moleskin trousers – which is the origin of the derogatory term 'blackleg' for a strike breaker.

Family folklore related that one of these Cornish miners, name unknown, was allegedly my great-great-granddad, thus giving my family the somewhat dubious distinction of being directly descended from one of the original 'blacklegs'.

This Cornishman fathered an illegitimate child (my great-granddad) with a young local girl by the name of Rachel Yates (born 1816, no date of death) who lived in Radcliffe. The child of this liaison was Thomas Yates (born 1835), who lived with his mother's family, taking his mother's family name, thus starting my branch of the family.

Thomas Yates married Ann Scholes in 1856 in Radcliffe and together they raised a family of nine children and adopted another three. The sixth-born was my granddad, William (born 1868). Most of the children emigrated to Canada, Australia and New Zealand, except my granddad and his brother Thompson. Thompson made himself a reasonable amount of money in cotton and steel and was able to financially help his siblings emigrate to what were then 'the colonies'.

Grandad's education was very brief, so much so that it finished at the age of nine, almost before it started. The school he attended was in Cocky Moor (Ainsworth) and was quite a walk from his home in the cottages.

The headmaster provided a lunch for those that had a long way to go home (for a price) and so Grandad stayed at school for lunch (or 'dinner' as it was referred to at the time). This lunch always consisted of a bowl of porridge or broth and recipients were charged one penny for the privilege, totalling five pence a week. This was no small sum at the time and, with other siblings to pay for, this proved quite an outlay for his struggling parents. Grandad, even at this tender age, had already developed a shrewdness and he was not impressed with this value for money.

"That weren't bloody porridge! It weren't even bloody gruel. Ah' seen 'im makin it, an it worn't wurth a penny. A handful o'thirds an' more salt t'take taste away, so ah' left skool reet away an' ah' ne'er went back," he proudly told me. And he didn't.

That same day he went to the local colliery (the Pretoria Pit, over Hulton Bolton) and got a job 'gal drivin'. This involved caring for and driving the pit ponies underground. In spite of the hardship, the pit ponies were generally well looked after and, although they were stabled and spent their working time underground, they were given regular 'holidays' in the fields above ground.

That was the start of his mining career. From looking after the ponies he soon progressed to a fully-fledged coal hewer, and apparently was a good collier. In the 1890s he could earn 35 shillings per day, which was good money for the job at the time. This career in the coal mine was to last quite a long time, and even though he could not read or write, he gained a terrific technical knowledge of mining.

For many years miners have been noted for their strong belief in upholding the tradition of 'Minus Monday'. They used to enjoy Saturday and Sunday to the full and recuperate on Monday, so on Mondays there was quite a lot of absenteeism.

Grandad became a very keen foot-follower of the local hunt and during the hunting season he never worked Saturdays or Wednesdays, these being the days when the Hunt met, and would spend much of his remaining spare time poaching. He soon became quite an accomplished poacher.

Ultimately, his passion for the Hunt probably saved his life. It was one Wednesday in the hunt season of 1910 that a terrific explosion in that part of the Pretoria Mine where my grandfather worked killed 344 miners, the third worst mining disaster in this country.

When questioned about his work colleagues, Grandad's retort was, "That was before thee wor' born, so what the 'ell does it matter now?" [Editor's Note: See Appendix A – 1. The Pretoria Pit Disaster.]

Why he was such a strong foot follower of the hunt I could never understand, but it seems to have got him well known – and while he was following the hunt over various parts of the countryside, he was keeping an eye open for the most profitable places to go poaching. I discovered this when I started to look for work when my schooldays was over and discovered how well and widely known he was and his reputation in poaching and hunting circles.

I never discovered exactly what he did to get so well known locally, but everyone seemed to have great respect for him. I also never discovered how he came by his nickname of 'Cherry'. The nearest I ever got to establishing the origin was when he was telling me about one of his escapades when he was younger and someone called him a 'cherry-nosed bugger'. The only time I could get him to talk about his early days was after he had consumed a few pints of Granny's elderberry wine.

On one such evening he swore in all sincerity that one night when he was returning home from the Three Arrows (a pub on the road between Bolton and Bury) he saw a 'bogart' climb on the fence that surrounded a clough, appropriately known locally as 'Bogart Hole Clough' (not to be confused with the Bogart Hole Clough in Blackley, Manchester), and he finished this story with, "An' I wurn't bloody drunk either!"

Grandad was devoted to his wife, Catherine Nuttall (born 1870). They married in 1890 and both worked very hard to maintain the household. She had three sisters, two of whom we saw every year at Christmas and New Year, the third I only vaguely remember seeing once.

It was midsummer and I remember this lady, very smart, but getting Grandma very angry about something. Being a small child at the time I did not understand what it was all about, but I do remember Grandma swearing, and I never heard her do that before or since. Apparently, the row was because Grandma's sister had told my mother, who was estranged from my father, that she should join him in Yorkshire. This prompted a reply from Grandma to "get back to bloody Australia where you belong, and don't ever come here again."

Whenever I visited Grandad's mother's house (my Great Grandmother, Ann) I was always intrigued by the trophies hung on nails knocked into the beams in the living room of her cottage. These trophies took the form of copper kettles and I always wondered why there were so many.

On one of my Grandad's 'wine evenings' I took the opportunity to ask why there were so many copper kettles hanging from the beams in his mother's house. I had to pick my moment, otherwise I would get the sharp response, "Mind thi' own bloody business!" which was his standard response to anybody who asked him a question he did not want to answer.

However, I had picked my moment correctly, and to my great delight and surprise he told me that every kettle was a 'trophy' of a fight, and went on to explain that his father fought in organized fights using fists and feet, known as "Punchin' Matches". These fights did not follow Queensbury Rules and the combatants wore special clogs, very light with no irons on the bottom as ordinary clogs had, and the upper leatherwork was usually a work of art, the owner taking great pride in his appearance.

The 'purse' to the winner was a £5 note, pushed into the spout of a copper kettle, but heavy betting on the side would also occur, with sums reaching £50, which was obviously illegal. At the time (mid-late 1800s) this was quite a sum for a working man; even the £5 was a fair return for a few minutes work, in spite of the risks.

When I asked him if he took part in any such fights, he gave me a look which made me wish I hadn't asked such a silly question. He then replied,

"Aye, Ah did. Not so much as mi Dad, but enough to learn to fight and to learn it wor' a mug's game. If mi Dad 'ad learnt it wor' a mug's game as well, he might have lived longer. He weren't so old when he died."

Great-Grandad (Thomas) was 56 when he died but Grandad, his brother Thompson and my great-grandmother all agreed that his dad's death was due to taking part in these fights.

When he died, Great-Grandma collected all the £5 trophies and bought herself a chip shop in Bury. Once she had established the shop she would work very hard for about three months, then would close the shop for a week and attempt to drink all the pubs in Bury dry. Generally, this resulted in the local police having to escort her home. After recovering from this binge she would not touch a drop until the next time, usually a couple of months later!

Apparently, when she contracted the illness which eventually claimed her life, she complained to the doctor who had been attending to her for some time, "Don't bring me no more of thy buggerin' medicine, I know what's wrong wi' me."

"And what do you think is wrong with you?" the doctor replied.

"I've gotten cancer! And next time thee comes, fotch mi a hafe ance o' baccy an a bottle o' Guinness."

And he did.

Whilst working at The Pit, Grandad took a shine to a young mining engineer by the name of Percy Shipperbottom. Percy worked with my Grandad, who mentored him, improving his mining skills and he helped Percy pass his under-manager's papers. He was a successful and talented mining engineer and Grandad brought this young man home and introduced him to his eldest daughter, Henrietta, and so romance blossomed between my parents.

Percy was also from a working-class mining family and worked with Grandad in the pit, but when I was a baby he secured a good job at a pit in Yorkshire. Once settled, he apparently invited my mother along with myself to join him in Yorkshire, but my mother, being a very stubborn woman, refused to leave her family and hence they parted and my mother and I lived with my mother's family.

The only mention my mother made of the Shipperbottom family was that Grandad Shipperbottom was a 'real gentleman'.

And so I was raised and mentored by my Grandad, William Yates.

❖ ❖ ❖

~ CHAPTER 2 ~

Early Years ~ 1915-22

I WILL TRY, GOING BACK MORE than 100 years, to describe the place where I was born and lived the first seven years of my life. Approximately two miles out of Bolton centre, along the road from Bolton to Bradshaw, the road crosses the river Tonge. At the far end of the bridge, a turning on the left led into Hypatia Street, this being the first of four streets which made up the 'Brookfield' area or, as it was known to the locals, 'The Glory Hole'.[1]

Walking along Hypatia Street, past the Dye Works on the left, the next street was Brookfield Street. This was the 'posh' street – bay windows with a pocket-size gardens at the front – and was looked upon with a level of respect by the rest of the populace of the Glory Hole, for the simple reason that the law was represented by the one policeman who lived there.

The next street was Gurth Street, a row of terraced houses typical of the area, which housed mainly working-class families on low or no income. The next street, Smethurst Street, where I was born, was also a terraced street, all the houses with outside tippler toilets, none had bathrooms; we lived at Number Six.

On the right-hand side of Hypatia Street was first a woodshed, then a fence made up of a row of old wooden sleepers. The reason for the fence eluded me because it never deterred anyone from going beyond it. Beyond the fence lay an area known as the 'Top Brow'. From there you could take a shortcut to the fields, the allotments or the local colliery, Tonge Colliery (known locally as 'Jet's Pit') all which lay just a short walk from there. This colliery featured significantly in my family history; Grandad

[1] *Editor's note*: Hypatia Street and Brookfield Street still exist but the other streets have been cleared.

helped to 'sink' that pit and my Uncle Wilfred worked there until its closure.

At the far end of the streets the gable ends of the terraces faced onto a dirt track which connected all the back streets. On the other side of the track was a slope known as 'Little Brow', which in turn led to a large area known as 'The Meadow'. Surrounding the Meadow was a brook, presumably thus creating the name for the area, 'Brookfield'. Across the Meadow lay the Bleachworks and Brickworks.

My Family and Early Childhood

I WILL NOW introduce you to my family, who lived in the house and raised and mentored me. This consisted of my maternal family, as my father had left to work in Yorkshire and my mother had refused to join him. My maternal family name was Yates. There was my Grandad, William Yates, his wife Catherine and their children in order of age: William (Uncle Bill), Henrietta (my mother), James (Our Jim), Sarah Ellen (Aunt Sarah) and Wilfred (Our Wilf). Wilf, being the youngest, was only some 15 years older than me and took on the role of an older brother, and would get annoyed if I called him Uncle!

My earliest clear memory is that of a large bonfire and everybody enjoying themselves, singing and chanting "It's over, the war is over!" The date was 11th November 1918 and I had just turned three years old.

Another clear childhood memory, a short time after this momentous event (for the country, not so relevant to me at the time) was playing with the other children on the slope near the brickworks. We played in gangs and built 'forts' with clinkers and bricks, from which we would charge another gang in their fort. During one such attack someone looked up and pointed to an airship overhead. One of the older boys shouted "Zeppelin!" and started to run home in fear. It was obviously not hostile, as the war was over, but Bolton had suffered air raids during the

Great War and this incident showed the instilled fear of an aerial attack in those early days.[1]

About this time (early 1919) a momentous, life-changing event occurred. A large (to my young eyes) motor van arrived at the front of our house. It was an army ambulance. Immediately a crowd gathered to see what was happening. First, two men got out, carrying with them a wheelchair. They helped a man out, who seemed to have some difficulty walking, even with two sticks. But walk he did, and into our house. One of the men pushed the empty wheelchair into the house and then, after a few words, the ambulance drove away.

'Our Jim' had finally come home from the War, minus two legs from above the knee. From that moment, from being a small child and for the rest of my life, I had the greatest respect and admiration for him, he was my idea of what makes a strong man, in stature if not in build. Many years later I carried him to his grave, but even now I still try to live up to the idea of his kind of being a man, in the real sense.

I say this because at the tender age of 22 years old he 'went over the top' during the battle at Passchendaele on 26th October 1917 and a shell burst near him. Both legs were shattered (the fibia and tibia) and because he was not found for two days, by then gangrene had set in and, despite the efforts of the surgeons, his left leg was amputated on 30th October 1917 and his right leg the next day. He suffered further complications after the amputations with 'leakages and bleeds' and was in Queen Mary's Military Hospital in Whalley until 24th October 1918, before being transferred to Bolton Infirmary. He was eventually sent home on 25th January 1919. But all this did not deter him from achieving many things many able-bodied men did not.

The next great event in my life was starting school. I was eager to start, as all my friends had already done so, and during schooldays I had no playmates. My friends told me how much they enjoyed school, so I gave my family no peace until it was

[1] See Appendix 2. Zeppelin Raid on Bolton 1914.

agreed I should go to school, even though I had not reached five years old, the normal accepted age to start school.

So the great day arrived and my special friend from Girth Street took me on my first day. An old man, I later discovered to be the headmaster, took me to the teacher who was in charge of the class known as 'The Fives'. From there one progressed to 'The Sixes' and then 'Standard One', which should be reached by the age of seven, an objective I proudly achieved.

Games and Pastimes

FOR ALL SMALL boys of that era, marbles took priority over other activities. The boy who had the largest bag of 'marps' (marbles) was well respected (the equivalent of today's 'street cred').

The main game was rolling one marble to the other; a hit was worth one and a hit and spin was worth two. This game was played with "iron dowdies", which were steel ball-bearings of various sizes, and "glass allies", which were obtained by breaking pop bottles which had a glass ball in the neck. Pay-outs were usually made with ordinary marbles; iron dowdies and glass alleys could be bartered against a number of ordinary marbles.

As marbles were a form of currency amongst my gang, I hit upon a brilliant idea. Instead of paying out with marbles I had paid good money for (twelve for one penny), why not make my own? If bricks could be made out of clay at the brickworks, why not marbles?

So off I went to the brickworks and helped myself to some clay. I took a great deal of care to make my marbles nice and round, then put them in the oven and baked them until I thought they were hard enough. I got out my paint box and painted them all different colours. When they had dried, I was in business!

All went well at first and I used them to 'pay out' when I lost games, but I was found out when they were used during a game called 'knock-out'. Knock-out was simply a rough circle drawn on the paving flags and a pyramid drawn in the centre, the object was to hit the pyramid and knock marbles out of the ring.

Unfortunately, my home-made marbles started to split. Apparently, I wasn't the first person to enter this entrepreneurial field. I was not aware of this fact and I certainly had to fight that day before I was allowed to go home. There were many other ways one could lose or win marbles, all of which at that time was serious to us.

But we soon discovered other things to life.

I think most of the boys in Brookfield learned to swim in a part of the river known as the "Sandy Bottoms". Some of the older boys would take the younger boys and watch that none of the learners got into difficulties. Of course, swimming trunks were a thing of the future, we only discovered them later when we started to go to the local swimming baths.

When we could satisfy our 'minders' that we could swim well enough, we were allowed to go with them to the local pit lodge. This was a lodge belonging to Jet's Pit and it somehow re-cycled water to the pit's boilers and therefore the water was always warm, winter and summer.

A high wall surrounded the lodge, but this presented no obstacle to us. We undressed on the outside of the wall and then scrambled over, leaving one or two non-swimmers on top of the wall to keep a watch on our clothes and for anyone whose task it was to keep children away from the lodge.

Occasionally we had to make a hasty exit, when we would grab our clothes and run to a field nearby, which seemed to vary its produce from grass to wheat, oats and swedes. We would dress in the field and if the swedes were in season, we would 'borrow' one. Someone always had the means to peel and cut it up and I will always remember how good a piece of that fresh swede tasted after a swim in the pit lodge.

The Bleachworks had an 'ash tip' where a cart came three or four times a day and tipped the ashes from the boiler-house. A favourite pastime for the 'Brookites' was to collect or 'pike' from the ashes any unburnt coal, cinders or anything else that would keep the home fires burning.

A much more risky but lucrative option was purloining coal from the pit yard, but this was a desperate measure because it was deemed as deliberate stealing, with all that would mean if caught, but some were desperate enough to take that risk.

From the pithead to the pit yard, a distance of approximately 200-300 yards, was a conveyor belt known as 'Waggon Road', which brought tubs of coal from the pit to the yard. It was while the coal was in transit on Waggon Road that the best opportunity presented itself for the brave to get the coal, although not many tried because it was too well patrolled.

As the men started to return home from the Great War, the Glory Hole took on the atmosphere for which it became known. A hard place with a very tight, secular community. A lot of the veterans, despite the horrors of the trenches and the hardships they had experienced, were still full of 'get up and go' and soon formed themselves into groups and societies such as pigeon fanciers, fishing clubs and even formed a football team called Brookfield United.

I became a great fan of theirs because I enjoyed football and even got myself the important job of carrying one of the player's bags and travelling with the team. I went to places I hadn't been to before (even though they were all in the locality of Bolton), which broadened my then very narrow horizons. But the most important reward was after the match, when the player whose bag I carried had put his gear back in the bag, he would give me threepence (3d) and tell me to take the bag straight home. Then he would go off with the rest of the team to their usual pub.

The Meadow became the home ground for the football team, but it also served as a venue for other recreational community activities. Rounders was very popular amongst families in those days and any girl who was good at rounders was usually offered a 'good job' at one of the local mills, provided she would play for that mill (by coincidence a policy used by American Colleges in later years for football, baseball or basketball players).

The referee in these games, as in today's football matches, was either a saint or a devil's advocate. I have witnessed many arguments and even fights over a bad decision by a rounders referee. My uncle Bill was a rounders referee and in the course of a season he was everything from a hero to a villain with the mind and brains of a louse!

Sunday mornings was the morning for 'piggy' matches. Much money changed hands on these, but the matches stopped when it was 'opening time' and the players would go for a celebration or consolation drink.

Two of the men who returned from the Great War played a major part in my life. One was Jim Monks, who courted my aunt Sara, whom he eventually married, and more importantly the other was Harry Pettigrew, who for many years (approximately 55 years!) courted my mother, who was still a very attractive young woman after she had parted from her husband. Whilst they had a very long term stable relationship, she never agreed to marry him, proving what a stubborn woman she was.[1]

All this time he visited her two or three times a week, always (as far as I know) returning home at the end of the evening, and he was like a father to me and later a grandfather to my children. He eventually suffered a stroke in the 1970s and became incapacitated, but even then, despite offers of my grown-up sons to take her to visit him, she refused. We never heard any more from him.[2]

From ever since I could remember, my Aunt Sara took me everywhere with her, even when she went out with Jim Monks.

---

[1] *Editor's note*: to my knowledge she never divorced her husband but she did get a 'separation order' in 1920.

[2] *Editor's note*: I always felt very sorry for Harry, because he never had a family of his own. I suppose he was waiting for my grandmother to agree to marry him. He was like a grandfather to me and my brothers, a quiet, kind man, such a gentleman!

Although he didn't actually lose his arm during the war, he was so badly injured that he was never able to hold a proper job. Because of his injuries he received a pension and because he could not work he could spend a lot of time at our house.

Very early I tested his sense of humour when they took me to the market one day. Outside one of the stalls was a stack of children's scooters, which were very popular with children at that time, and I saw a chance of making a show among the other kids with a 'posh' new scooter. No-one stopped me from trying the scooter, so off I 'scooted', with my Aunt Sara chasing me, shouting for me to come back, but I kept on going all the way home. Aunt Sara scolded Jim Monks for paying for the 'stolen' scooter his future nephew had absconded with, but fortunately for me he did think it quite funny.

Soon after our Jim came home, many things seemed to happen. From the paved part of the back street a large piece of ground reached almost to the brickworks and, since no-one seem to object, we acquired sole use of it. First of all a fence and wire-netting was put up, then Grandad, Our Wilf, Our Jim, Harry Pettigrew and Jim Monks were all kept very busy sawing and hammering, and soon we had hens and even a pony and trap.

It didn't end there, despite the storage space needed for food (a low priority, apparently) there still stood two empty sheds. This situation did not last for very long because a 'Scott' motorcycle and sidecar soon made its appearance; this machine would be worth a fortune today. Being all hand-controlled, Our Jim could drive it, so he and Wilf drove it between them.

They made quite a name for themselves because they always seemed to come roaring round the top of the meadow when there was a rounders match in progress and quite a crowd watching. But to me the motorcycle seemed to spend more time in pieces on the floor. I know that Grandma used to carry on at them frequently when they took bits off her sewing machine to repair some part of the engine!

These 'mechanical lessons' were good experience for me when I got my own motorbike some years later. Even then, if I could not get my bike to run smoothly I would take it to our Jim and he would fix it in no time.

Poacher's Apprentice and Other Experiences

WHEN I WAS about six years old Grandad decided that I was old enough to learn the art of poaching. On that first expedition we went right out in the country, to me it seemed like miles into a completely alien world because I had hardly been out of the local area of terraced houses. Grandad wore a jacket with massive pockets, known as 'poacher's pockets'. In one pocket he had nets and in the other he had a bag containing a ferret.

In the hedgerow of one of the fields he knelt to look at a hole, then went a little further to another hole. I didn't know it at the time, but I was looking at my first rabbit hole. Taking a net out of his pocket he said, "This is 'ow t' set a pus [purse] net."

Then he found another hole and gave me a net saying, "Now thee do it."

After one or two attempts I laid the net to his satisfaction, then he said, "Reet, thee stop 'ere an' ah'll put ferret in down theer. If a rabbit comes out thee grab it an' 'ang on to it. Ah'll get t' thee quick as I con, but fer Christ's sake don't let it goo."

Then he went to the first hole, put the ferret in, quickly put a net over that hole and seated himself between the first two holes. In what seemed a very short time a rabbit bolted out of the second hole and Grandad dealt with it very quickly.

Then, it seemed almost seconds later, a rabbit bolted into the net where I was. With difficulty I grabbed the rabbit and net and a third rabbit managed to run free. Grandad quickly dealt with the rabbit I was hanging on to and a second later the ferret appeared. I picked up the ferret and Grandad took it from me, putting the ferret in its bag and then into his pocket. One of the rabbits and nets went into the other pocket. He then pointed to 'my' rabbit, saying, "Thee carry that."

So off we went, a very brave six-year-old after his first experience in the art of poaching. We were about half way home when it started to rain and soon it was torrential, with thunder and lightning. We stood under a tree and Grandad tried to cover my shoulders with some of his coat.

Then there was such a terrible crack of thunder and a flash of lightning that seemed to come right down to us. What did come down was a branch of a tree next to us and Grandad looked at the large branch and said, coining a phrase made famous by John Wayne, "Ah think we 'ad better get t'ell out o'ere. C'mon Pea, ah'll carry that rabbit and thee owd ont' my 'and."

So, holding Grandad's hand, I returned triumphantly home from my first poaching lesson.

For my seventh birthday I was bought a bicycle and Our Wilf, Jim Monks and Harry took it in turns to teach me to ride it. The bike had an 18-inch frame and 26-inch wheels. Even with the saddle down to the bottom I could hardly reach the pedals, so Wilf put some wooden blocks on them so I could reach them.[1]

I must have been a very frustrating pupil for my teachers and between them they must have run miles round and round the meadow, holding the back of the saddle, but every time they let go of me, I fell off. After nearly a week of this, Our Jim, who had been watching operations from the top of the meadow, declared that if I didn't ride the bike by the next day, it would have to go back.

This ultimatum made me very determined. After all, besides losing the bike, I would lose face among my mates, to whom I had been boasting about my new bike and half promised to let one or two have a ride. To have a bike of your own at that age was something in those days.

On the day of test, I gripped the handlebars, gritted my teeth and made a very determined but very wobbly solo circuit of the

---

[1] *Editor's note*: A service Uncle Wilf also undertook for me when I was given my first adult bike at about the same age and couldn't reach the pedals either!

meadow. Our Wilf and Harry, grinning like two Cheshire cats, shouted to Our Jim, who was at top of the meadow,

"Will he do?"

"He's not bloody safe yet. Keep it going 'til he c'n ride it proper," Jim replied.

So round and round that meadow I rode, until my legs was tired and I knew every blade of grass. Our Wilf and Harry had sneaked off for a pint but I daren't stop until I was told to, too much was at stake for me. Eventually they reappeared.

"Reet Pea..." I was always called Pea. "Come on out o' meadow and let's see what you are like ont' streets."

So round and round the streets I rode, twisting and turning, up backstreets, up and down front streets. I didn't mind this too much because some of my gang were watching and I felt good waving to them as I rode past. Eventually our Jim came to the front door and stopped me.

"Reet Pea... that'll do!"

The wheelchair Our Jim had been provided with was propelled by a system of two levers; one had a handgrip to steer with and the levers, when worked backwards and forwards in turn, worked a system which propelled the rear wheels. This was very hard work if any reasonable distance was to be covered.

One Sunday morning – I remember it being a Sunday even after all these years because the events of that morning set a precedent which was to last until I was 15 years old, long after Jim had received a better, more efficient form of mobility – after I had got up and our Jim had his breakfast, Jim told me to 'get a move on'. When I asked why, he just grinned and told me we were going 'for a ride'.

I needed no further encouragement and must have broken all records getting ready. We soon set off, me proudly riding my bike and following Our Jim down the street on the first of many such trips. When we got to Bury Road he turned left towards Bury, which put us at the foot of a hill which led to Tonge Fold. I got to the top of the hill, left my bike there and ran back to help Jim and push him up the hill. I enjoyed this, in spite of the hard work required, because I was proud of Our Jim and liked to think my childish efforts helped him. At least he seemed to appreciate my help.

We continued towards Bury until we came to the Three Arrows pub, where we turned left until we came to a dirt road which led to a row of three cottages with fields all around and a large garden in the front. All this has now gone in the path of progress, but then it was a charming quiet place and there lived a very lively old lady who welcomed us in the traditional way with a pot of tea and homemade cake. The lady was my Grandad's mother, Our Jim's grandmother and my great grandmother. After this day I visited her every Sunday until her death, when I was fifteen and she was over ninety.

Every Sunday when I visited her, she always greeted me with "How's our Will?"

She spoke in a very broad Lancashire dialect, which I will not attempt to repeat in words. Her question was about my Grandad, her son. I was greeted with this comment even if Grandad had visited her only the day before.

Then she always asked me if I had time to run an errand for her. I would say I had and then she would give me some money, and say. "Go t' Starnall and get me half ounce o' baccy. Make sure it's twist mind thee."

When I returned with her 'baccy', thin twist it was, I was then allowed to go in the garden and pick an apple or pear if it was summer – "Only one, mind thee!" – and I had to prove I only had one.

In winter she would produce an apple from the kitchen. I would then have tea and cake and after a while she would say, "They'll all be worried 'bout thee. Thee 'ad better be off."

Childhood & Early Teens – 1922–1930

I WAS DOING well at school and gaining experience of life in other spheres of activity. On Saturday mornings four or five of us had started to go to Bridgeman Street baths in Bolton. For threepence we had entry to the baths and hire of 'towel and drawers'. (No more swimming in the Sandy Bottoms or Pit Lodge naked as the day we were born, we had started to behave a little more mature!) But there were other benefits to be gained from our visits to the swimming baths.

On entering the baths, if you were lucky enough, you could get a cubicle to change into the 'borrowed' drawers (swimming trunks). More often than not we were ordered by one of the two tough attendants to change 'up there' – 'up there' being the gallery. Kids had to leave the cubicles vacant for the 'grown ups'. In those days there were a lot of miners in the area and on Saturday mornings they came to the baths for a good scrub down and a swim before they went to their usual local. These were the 'grown-ups' we had to save the cubicles for.

For obvious health reasons, before anyone could go into the large swimming pool, one had to make use of the 'little plunge' or 'slipper bath'. This was a communal hot bath which everyone had to use, and also make use of the large block of carbolic soap and very stiff scrubbing brush, under the watchful eye of one of the attendants. From there one had to go under the cold shower, still under the eye of the attendant. and then, and only then, could one dive into the main plunge and swim.

When the miners came in, they would scrub themselves, but they could not thoroughly scrub their backs. Then they would shout to one of us, "Hey kid, come an' do mi' back for me."

Gladly, one of us would take up the chore, in spite of the chivvying we would receive from the miners to make us put more effort into our labours, with such remarks as, "Come on kid, put some weight in it, what did thee 'ave for breakfast?"

We would try to comply, even though sweat was pouring off us, and that soap and scrubbing brush felt like a ton weight, but we always got a penny for our trouble and, as the miners were leaving, they would throw pennies into the main plunge for us to dive for.

When we came out of the baths we would count up our pennies and, more often than not, we could afford to buy a 'penny mile' each from the cake shop across the road from the baths. This was a homemade three-cornered wedge of currant cake, so long that our arms were at full extent when we started to eat it.

Having devoured the penny mile, we would make our way as fast as we could to the tripe shop near Tonge Bridge, where we would buy a pennyworth of tripe bits. At that time sweets and toffee never entered our thoughts. If the weather was not so good, I would go with the gang to the 'penny rush' at the local cinema, but more often than not I would go for a ride on my bike.

The Jumbles and its Surrounding Area

THINGS HAD SETTLED into a routine. Granny was doing well selling eggs to the neighbours, Great Grandma's chip shop in Bury had come under the family influence (funded by her husband's fighting trophies) and, as far I was concerned, everything was settled and comfortable. But then came the big change...

I came home from school one day and Grandad said, "You can tell your teacher that you will be leaving school next week."

This surprised and worried me a little because the main reason children at my age were taken out of school is because they were being sent to Reform School. When I asked why, he just replied, "We are moving."

Again I wanted to know why, to which he replied, "I've got a job as a gamekeeper, so we 'ave to move 'cause o' t'job."

I was mystified and wanted to know what a 'gamekeeper' was.

"He's a kind o' policeman, so thee had better watch thee P's and Q's in future," Jim teased. "He looks after different birds an' fish an' such, an' protects 'em from people like poachers. He's like a policeman 'an can stop 'em from stealin' an' can bring 'em t'court if he catches 'em poaching."

Now I was confused! Especially after learning and partaking in Grandad's 'hobby'. How could Grandad be a poacher *and* a gamekeeper?

Jim could see my consternation, but Grandad was laughing and added, "Don't thee worry thee sen lad, the'll enjoy it wur we'r gooin'."

Feeling a bit more relieved, I asked, "Where's that?"

"A place called t' Jumbles. It's a house on it's own an' thee'll be goin' to a school in Bradshaw."

Feeling a little more relieved I was now wondering how could I explain it to my teacher in the morning?

But I needn't have worried the teacher told me she understood, wished me well and said I could have the rest of the time off to help to get ready for moving.

Everything seemed to happen at once. The pony and trap disappeared, my Granny's hens went and the chip shop had new owners. All I know is that on the day for moving all final preparations were in place.

After breakfast our Jim said, "Why don't you go on, Pea? Our Wilf's already there."

He instructed me very carefully how to get to our new place of abode and although I followed those instructions to the letter, I finished up following a path through a field. All I could see in the distance was trees and no sign of the house our Jim said I should see. Instead all I could see was a lot of nosey cows making their way towards me.

Not being well versed in country life at the time, I beat a hasty retreat, all the way back to Brookfield. I was just in time to catch the moving van and put my bike on the back. Our Jim roared with laughter when I told him about my 'adventure'. Apparently, I had turned back no more than 200 yards from the house, which couldn't be seen because of all the trees in full leaf.

I will describe the area which was to be my new home as it is now and how it used to be. The Jumbles is now a reservoir and is situated in a valley off Bradshaw Road between Bradshaw and Turton. Travelling north out of Bolton to Bradshaw turn left at Bradshaw Church, approximately half a mile on the left are some trees and a wall just before the entrance to Bradshaw industrial units.

These units are what is left of Bradshaw Bleachworks, which used to 'bus in' hundreds of workers every day. Behind the trees is a stone doorway, which for some reason has been left as a monument to what used to be Bradshaw Hall, where Colonel Hardcastle, Grandad's employer, used to live. It has always puzzled me as to why they left the doorway standing because it cannot been seen from the road due to the trees.

As the road rises and bends away from what used to be the Bleachworks there is a sharp bend to the left and after approximately another half mile is a dirt track on the left. This was the only access to The Jumbles, our new abode. The track dipped away into the valley and had a few bends in it and all this was covered by thick woodland. To the left the valley drops away sharply down to the brook at the bottom. [See Appendix 3 – The Gamekeeper's Cottage, The Jumbles.]

On the left at the top of the track there were some fields and at the bottom were the lodges, which fed water to the Bleachworks and were the responsibility of the Gamekeeper. This area used to teem with wildlife of all kinds. As you neared the end of the track on the right was 'the quarry'. This consisted of sandstone cliffs which created a sheltered semi-circle. Just past the quarry on the right was the entrance to the Gamekeeper's cottage.

As you entered the double gate there was a paved area which gave access to all the different outbuildings. On the right was the coal scullery, the ash pit and the tippler toilet. The house never had any mains services whatsoever. On the left of the paved area was a small rose garden and then the main house. It was an old beamed stone house with deep window sills. As you entered on the right was the 'best room', only used for weddings, funerals, etc. On the left was the main room and behind that the kitchen.

Off the kitchen were the stairs to four bedrooms. Lighting was provided by storm lamps. The fire had a cooking range attached to it and heated the water, which was piped and filtered from the quarry behind the house.

Back outside at the end of the paved area were some steps which led up to the wash-house, workrooms and the 'back plantation'.

Outside the gate, back on the track, the track narrowed into a path which went over a bridge over the small brook which ran past the house. To the left the path dropped down to the main river and the bridge over the river led to a path across the fields, which eventually came out into Shady Lane, Bromley Cross.

Sharp left from the track there was a gate which had the sign 'Private Path'. This path ran alongside the valley to the lodges and finally came out at the Bleachworks. Turning right along the path outside the house ran along the brook and if followed all the way, approximately two miles, came out of the woods, across some fields, went past the waterfall and came out eventually at the Horrobin in Turton Bottoms.

All this area was beautiful woodland but now from just past where the house stood up to the Horrobin is now under a reservoir. The house has been pulled down because it wasn't considered safe to live under a large dam. The last people to live in the house were Our Wilf and his wife Florence.

Having described the area I hope you can now visualize some of the events I am about to relate.

So began my new way of life, a life I enjoyed to the full over the years to come, and although I still kept in touch with the Brookfield crowd, I grew more and more away from them as the years passed. Being young, I soon adapted to the change of lifestyle and all it entailed. When we lived in Brookfield we had two dogs, but very soon after we moved to the Jumbles we had two more, a Golden Labrador and an Irish Water Spaniel, these dogs I soon learned were gun dogs.

My Gran's livestock soon increased from a few hens to turkeys, geese, ducks and soon pigs. All this meant I had to earn my living by doing a few extra chores. I had to take some part in the care and maintenance of the livestock, which consisted mainly of cleaning out their various abodes. I got really fond of the pigs and made pets of them, so when the pork butcher came, I disappeared for the day.

Another chore was to take eggs to Gran's customers in Brookfield. That worked in very well for me because after I had delivered the eggs I could go to the Lads' Club with one or two of my mates.

But one Friday I didn't make it.

It was a winter's night and a very heavy fog came down. I used to take the eggs on the handlebars of the bike and to get up the lane to the main road there was a small footpath which ran along the edge of the lane and the plantation, down which was a very steep incline. Confident I could find that patch of smooth path with my eyes closed, I pedalled as fast as I could... and missed the path.

The bike, eggs and self all tumbled down the steep incline, somehow missing the trees, but the eggs was of no further use. Needless to say, I didn't go out that night and the eggs had to be delivered the following morning.

Owd Harry

THE FIRST OF my daily chores was to go for the milk. In the morning I went to a farm across the field at the back of the house and for the evening milk I had to go to another farm very close to the first farm. But the second farm was also a pub, run by two brothers known as 'Owd Harry' and 'Owd John'. The pub was known simply as Owd Harry's. [Editor's note: This later became 'The Lamb Inn' on Bradshaw Road for many years and now I think it is a Chinese Restaurant.]

After I had been going for the evening milk a few days, Owd Harry asked, "Ow's thee like livin' at Bradshaw Mill?" I was more than puzzled by the question.

"It's Gamekeepers Cottage we live at, not Bradshaw Mill," I replied, "an' I like it very much."

He laughed. "Aye lad, Gamkeeper's Cottage it might be now, but long afore that it were Bradshaw Corn Mill. Thee ask Owd Cherry, he'll tell thee."

Again I was puzzled. "Who's Owd Cherry?"

"Bloody 'ell lad! Dus't not know thi own Grondfather? That's who Owd Cherry is!"

At this point I decided that I needed a lot more information that this talkative old farmer seemed to have about Grandad, and perhaps he might even know how Grandad got his gamekeeper's job and house and everything.

"Have you known mi Grandad long?" I asked.

"Aye lad, long afore thee wur thowt on, ne'er mind born and Owd Marci."

"Who's Marci?" I asked.

"Why, thi grondfathers' gaffer, owd 'Ardcastle. Major 'e wur then, an thy Gronfather wur comin' up road an' just getten t'that gate theer, con see just down theer? An Marci on his 'orse wanted go thru t'gate t'gerrin t'Jumbles. He towd thi Grondfather t'open t'gate. Anyhow, Owd Cherry towd Marci to open it 'is bloody self!"

Well, Marci lashed out at Owd Cherry, an' what did Owd Cherry do? Why, he grabbed t'whip wi one hand, an' Marci wi' t'other an' bye gow didn't Owd Cherry lather t'Major, an when he'd done, he helped t'Major back on t'orse, opened gate fer 'im an' said t' Major, "Next bloody time be a bit more p'leet!' I stood wur we are naw an seed an' 'eard it all."

Owd Harry continued, "Thi Grondfather wor a bloody 'ard man in them days, an' best bloody poacher in t' district!"

The number of times I was told about Grandad's poaching abilities in the years to come was amazing. The other constant label I received was "Thee one o' Owd Cherry's lads? Bloody dayleet poacher, nay bloody gamekeeper!'

I decided to go home and not say a word to Grandad, except to try and clear up if we lived at the Gamekeeper's Cottage or Bradshaw Mill. When I asked Grandad about the name of the house he told me that many years ago it was Bradshaw Mill and farmers from miles around would come to it. We went into what was termed the 'back plantation' and Grandad pointed out the traces of an old cart track that the farmers used to use to get to the mill.

Standing Up for Myself

I HAD QUITE a way to go to school but the school was not as big as the one I had left. I reported to the headmaster and when I told him I was in Standard One he told the teacher to give me a test. The result of that test was that I was immediately put into Standard Three. From Standard Three I moved to Standard Five and so on and by the time I was twelve I was in what was known as Ex-Seven.

So for two years I was one of the elite of four or five who had gone through the school curriculum and got extra teaching from the headmaster. In addition we also got some pleasant jobs to do, such as arranging football and cricket matches with other schools.

However, before I attained this pleasant level of school life, I had to go through a few ups, and downs. When I started that school I very soon found out that a gamekeeper was not a very popular person with some of the village residents, and that feeling reached out to the younger members of the family.

To "bash the gamekeeper's lad" was the right and proper thing to do and this situation lasted quite a long time until I proved that I wasn't quite so easy to 'bash'. I had started to go to the Lads' Club in Bolton, where my sole interest was boxing. In fact, from the age of seven to seventeen I went twice a week.

Two farmer's sons thought it great sport to set on me when I was on my way home from school and I seemed to get even more attention from them when I got to Standard Seven, at the age of eleven. These two brothers were both bigger and older than I was and there did not seem to be anything I could do, only fight back as well as I could. One day I came home in a bit of a mess and our Jim said I should "fetch 'em down to thy size". When I asked him how I could do that he said, "Hit 'em wi' thi bloody bike!"

I used to go to school on my bike. Now anything our Jim said to me or told me to do, I took literally, so I tried to work out how to hit two blokes with my bike.

Near our house was the old Quarry (the approach road to the quarry was still there until recently). Hour after hour I spent riding down the track and practicing in one smooth movement jumping off the bike, picking the bike up and swinging it in a half circle about one foot from the ground. I must admit I sustained many bruises on my shins and ankles before I got the movement to perfection, and eventually I judged I had got the movement just right, according to our Jim's instructions.

Two days later came the test, as I approached the lane that led to their farm they were waiting for me. I heard the youngest boy say, "Come on, let's get gamekeeper's lad."

I rode towards them slowly, judged the distance and then carried out what I had been rehearsing for days. It worked perfectly. With one swoop I had knocked both of them down, then I completed the last part of our Jim's instructions and 'went in with both feet'. In those days clogs was the general everyday footwear. Then I beat a hasty retreat, remembering the maxim, 'He who fights and runs away, lives to fight another day.'

But this action started a chain of events. First, the father of the two brothers came to our house, breathing fire and thunder. He threatened me with all kinds of violence if my Grandad didn't take action. He said that his sons would have to stay off school (which they did for three days) and that I was 'a nowty young bugger'.

Grandad heard him out and then said, very quietly, "When thy lads were belting 'im it was all reet, thee didn't stop 'em and he didn't complain, so we ne'er bothered. Now clog's on t'other foot thee'll not touch that lad an' I'll not touch thee. Now gerrup that road afore I put mi foot up thy arse!"

That was the longest speech I ever heard Grandad say.

When the two brothers came back to school the first thing the youngest did was to come to me and ask me if I would like to play in the school football team. I was more than pleased to say yes. We three then became good friends and so did the other farmer's sons in the school and strangely enough I never had to have another fight at school.

Our Very Own Coal Mine

WITH A VIEW to making a home for his family, Our Jim bought two acres of ground at the nearby village of Affetside. He obtained a caravan, so he had a temporary place to live and to work from. By this time his mobility had improved by virtue of the fact that he now had a motorised chair.

The family and a friend all helped to build a wooden bungalow raised about two feet from the ground. It was nearly finished when one night there was a very strong wind and the following morning I went up to his house with Grandad. Our Wilf and our Jim were already there, they had stayed in the caravan and when we arrived our Wilf was busy gathering the pieces of the bungalow which had been spread over the nearby fields.

Our Jim said that the next bungalow would not blow away. He was right. First of all he built a huge windbreak of sods and earth. Then the main uprights and the floor was sunk in concrete. When it was finished that bungalow stood up to all kinds of wind and weather for years.

For water he engaged the services of a water diviner, who walked around with his hazel twig, and you can take my word for it when I say that it worked. He told Our Jim where to sink a well and when Our Wilf did so, he eventually found water. Our Jim took a sample to the public analyst, who passed it as quite good quality and fit for human use. So a hand pump was fitted, which had to be primed before one could pump the water from down below, but Our Jim could now move in and set up home.

Lots of unusual things started to happen after Jim moved. The General Strike had already started (May 1926), I can remember the bus companies that defied the strike had to have the driver's cab protected by barbed wire or a policeman riding onboard to protect the crew.

At first the strike did not really affect us, except that Our Wilf, who still worked at Jet's Pit, was on strike. That was how Our Wilf could spend so much time helping Our Jim with his bungalow. But then the landscape going up the fields to our Jim's abode changed.

The miners from the town started to dig for outcrop coal and, to use the words of Harry Pettigrew, Our Jim and Jim Monks, 'it looked like Flanders'. After a few weeks Our Jim told Grandad that he thought of digging for coal. Grandad told him to forget the outcrop and that there was some old mine workings lower down, where there was a two foot seam of good coal.

Our Wilf started to sink the shaft and when he got a good distance down he had to fit a ladder. Then he came to rock, hard and seemingly impassable. Again, Grandad came to the rescue.

He told me to get on my bike and go to a sports shop in Withy Grove, Manchester for two pounds of black powder and a ring of fuse. Just imagine today, a kid of eleven cycling twelve miles to the busiest part of Manchester on a pushbike to buy gunpowder and a fuse and then bringing it the twelve miles back. It was a good job I had done quite a lot of cycle rides with our Wilf before that.

The following morning, I got up early; I wanted to see this blasting effort! I went up with Grandad and when we got there Our Wilf was banging away with a crowbar and a hammer, grunting, swearing mildly and sweating a lot, but not making much impression on the rock.

Grandad said that he would have a go, so Wilf, giving way to experience, climbed up the ladder. Grandad, taking off his coat, asked Our Jim for two cold chisels, which Jim produced from his stock of tools, and soon Grandad descended the ladder with chisels, fuse, gunpowder, a bobbin of cotton and some toffee bags.

In quick time he had made holes in the rock. He poured the black powder into the toffee bags, inserted a fuse, which he had cut into lengths, placed the bags into the holes, then packed them up with clay. After picking up his tools he lit the fuses and climbed out of the hole.

He stood back a little way from the hole and lit his pipe. After what seemed a long time there was a series of explosions. Grandad waited a minute or two and then said, "Reet... let's see what we've done."

I can see it now, three to four feet of rock, cut in a perfect square and below that... blackness. Grandad had successfully broken into the old workings he had talked about.

Our Wilf went down to clear away the debris and fitted the ladder firmly to the bottom of the shaft. Then we all went down to inspect, Grandad, Wilf, myself and lastly (much to our surprise) Our Jim, who had taken off his artificial legs and came down the ladder using just his hands (he later went back up the same way).

We went along a tunnel, about three feet from roof to floor, and on either side were pillars of coal, from the floor to the rock roof. Then we came to where a seam of coal faced us. My Grandad explained that when the seam was being worked, many years ago, a method of mining known as 'pillar and stall' had been used. No props were needed, as strategic columns of coal were left to support the roof.

In a day or so all was ready to start getting the coal out. A winch was fitted to wind the coal up to the surface in wooden boxes known as 'tubs' which had no wheels and were dragged or 'skidded' from where the coal was dug out to the bottom of the shaft. That part of the operation was mine, which I did for a few days. It was hard work, but I had to do my bit.

One morning Our Wilf decided to 'explore' and find out how far the coalface went. I eagerly went with him on the expedition. We had gone quite a distance when, to our surprise, we saw a light coming towards us. Behind the light was what seemed to me to be a very old man. This obviously startled us, me especially, but not apparently Our Wilf.

"Na then, you're not under Jimmy Yates's ground now,' the old man said to him.

I didn't follow most of the resulting conversation as I was too amazed that it was possible to encounter anyone so far underground in a 'deserted' mineshaft and how this old man could tell exactly where we were. I do know that arrangements were made to meet him in the pub, because he wanted a word with Grandad.

When our Wilf told Grandad of the encounter, all he said was, "Is that owd bugger still going?"

It seemed that that the 'owd bugger' had worked in that particular mine from when he was a boy up to the mine closing. The planned meeting at the pub later spelled the end of my days as a child mine worker.

At the meeting were Grandad, the 'owd bugger', Our Jim, Our Wilf and two mates of Wilf's from Jet's Pit. A good working agreement was come to, a consortium was set up, and Our Jim (whose land it was, after all) did well selling the coal. In fact, this enterprise lasted for up to six months after the general strike finished!

The saga of the mine had one final twist. On 7th May 1994 the *Bolton Evening News* ran a story about a Jim Francis, who owned the land, discovered the mineshaft and, for safety asked the Coal Board to fill it in and seal it once and for all. Ironically, he was writing a history of the local coal mines. If only he knew some of its real history!

School and Other Chores

BACK TO SCHOOL life. I had turned 12 years of age and, as mentioned, became an Ex-Seven. The headmaster took us on various subjects, such as maths, science and any subject we may have a special aptitude for. By accident I got interested in reading and my choice and enjoyment of reading improved.

What in the lower classes was called 'composition' now became 'essay' and we could pick our own subjects. My choice for that day was 'Spring'. I don't know why I picked that, but on just over a page I had written a masterpiece, at least, that is what the headmaster said when he read it out to those in Standard Seven.

The reading of the essay was the start of more notable events. I had finished that essay in quick time and then took out of my pocket a Sexton Blake novel I had 'borrowed' from Our Wilf. I got so engrossed in the adventures of Sexton Blake and his assistant Tinker that I never noticed the Headmaster walking round, or that he was stood behind me to see what I was writing, which I wasn't.

He picked up the book, glanced at it, and then seemed very pleased with my essay. He asked me if I enjoyed reading, to which I obviously replied yes. Then taking the Sexton Blake novel he said, "Call at my house on your way home after school, you can have this back and I will show you some reading material that you might find more interesting".

That was the start of my knowledge of good reading, sourced from the headmaster's personal library, which was to continue, on and off, for the next five years. The headmaster had the largest private library I had ever seen, and I did my best to read all of it. A hopeless task, because a lot of the books belonged to his brother, who was a doctor.

I seem to have led a very busy life at that time. I did a lot of cycling, mostly with Our Wilf, who introduced me to the Yorkshire Dales, which I never got tired of.

For the first two years Grandad used to go to Bradshaw Hall for his wages and he didn't need to sign for them, just make his 'mark'. Then a certain Major Besketh, whose family had a cotton mill, took over the post of Hunt Secretary and Grandad had to go to the mill for his monthly pay and had to sign his name to receive his money.

When my Gran read the letter to him he cursed in such a manner that any Forces Drill N.C.O. would have been proud of, he finished with, "Ow the bloody hell can ah sign mi name when ah can't even write?"

Gran, ever wise, came up with the solution. "Thee'll larn. Our Pea'll teach thee."

So, in my best schoolboy handwriting, I wrote *William Yates* and said, "Just copy that, Grandad."

He held the pencil, looked at the paper for a full minute, then said despairingly, "Ah'll ne'er be able t' do it".

So I put my hand on top of his and said, "Let me show you 'ow." And slowly I guided his hand to write his name.

After a few times, when he seemed a little more relaxed, I let go and said, "There y'are, it's easy. Now do it a few times every day without my help an' you'll be champion."

So at last Grandad learned to write, taught by his grandson. Probably not a unique situation at the time.

Grandad used to take me out with him quite a lot and he taught me country lore from a poacher's and now gamekeeper's point of view. I became very interested in this and started to read all the books I could.

He also taught me the art of dry stone walling. The reason for this was that where the hunt had been in the winter season the farmers always complained that the hunt had broken fences or knocked walls down and Grandad had to go and investigate and repair the walls where necessary.

A large area of the land by the house Grandad fenced in to make a vegetable garden and a rose garden. Another small chore I had to do was to put newspapers round all the base of the rose trees to catch the petals from the flowers as they fell. Gran made rose-petal wine from these.

She also made elderflower and wild berry wine. Again, it was my chore to collect washing baskets full of the flowers and berries.

In the summer months Gran opened a sweet shop. She sold sweets, cigarettes, jugs of tea and hot water, minerals and her home-made herb beer. My Grandad used to take me out and show me what herbs to collect. Of course all this activity, along with the usual household work, was a lot to do, so she paid some of her Brookfield friends to help out.

It always seemed to be cold dark nights when she put eggs in the incubator to hatch out her chicks. Again I came in useful, I held the torch whilst Gran looked for 'first clears' (eggs that hadn't struck or hadn't started to form a chick).

She marked all those that had struck with a blob of blue dye and regularly she would go to the incubator armed with a bowl of water, warmed to just the right temperature. She took each egg and gently put it in the water. The result of that exercise told her if an egg was addled or not.

The blue mark told her how much she had to turn the eggs. That done, she cleaned and trimmed the paraffin heaters. When the chicks hatched, she put them in a paraffin heated brooder, where the chicks spent the first three or four weeks of their lives.

The 'first clears' she sold to the local village baker to use in his cakes and pastries. The first addled she boiled thoroughly and then mixed in with the mash she fed to the laying hens.

A Grim Discovery

WHAT WE CALLED the 'Second Jumbles' or 'Turton Jumbles' started past the Horribin Bleachworks. One day a friend and I, following the brook up towards Turton, decided to investigate what we thought was a cave we had often noticed before, but this time we brought a torch so we could go further in than the entrance.

As we got in, I noticed that the roof was propped, so I expected to come to some coal (now being an expert on these things from my time in Our Jim's pit!) but instead our torches picked out a man who appeared to be asleep but on closer examination we thought might be dead.

My Boy Scout training, scrappy though it was, told me to get out of there quick and inform somebody who was more capable of dealing with it. In my opinion nobody was more able to fit the bill than Grandad, so we broke all records back to our house. When I told Grandad he just asked me two questions. The first was "Ar't sure?" and second was "What the bloody 'ell was thee doin' theer anyway?"

Our Wilf and Grandad went off in a hurry, with two dogs and strict instructions, "You two young buggers don't move till we come back."

After what seemed hours of waiting, they returned. Our Wilf explained. "Aye, he's a stiff un' alreet. We left Bradshaw police and Turton police arguin' who has to shift 'im!"

Strangely enough, we never heard any more about it.

Learning to drive

ANOTHER OUTSTANDING MEMORY of 1927 was that I learned to drive. One of the farmer's sons I was friendly with asked me up one day with some of the local lads and intended to have a game of football in the pasture. Just a kick about, but it didn't work out that way, only one other boy turned up to play and he didn't stay too long and the lad who asked me up was found some chores to do by his dad.

I was about to go home when the farm labourer asked me if I'd like to help him to chain-harrow. Having never done that before I jumped at that chance, but much to my surprise he went to a motor with no top to it and gave me instructions how to start it. Then he told me to jump in and 'hang on', which I did, hung on like grim death on that bumpy ride across the field to the chain harrow.

After hooking up, he started the usual methodical treatment of the field, then he asked me if I'd like to 'have a go'. With him beside me, giving encouragement, I finished the field. After unhooking the harrow he allowed me to drive the tractor back to the farm. After that, I went up every chance I got to improve my driving skills, albeit on a tractor. The farm was probably one of the first in the area to use mechanized agricultural implements. The 'tractor'? That was an early Model T Ford with solid tyres.

The experiences on the farm increased my longing to drive 'properly'. Obviously, I was still five years under the legal age to obtain a proper driving licence, but that didn't deter me from driving and by the time I was of legal age I had driven three types of cars.

Strangely enough, by that time I was old enough to obtain a car licence my enthusiasm for motor cars had faded because I became the proud owner of a motorcycle. I had told my mother about a motorbike a friend of mine was selling for ten quid. Much to my delight my mother said I could have it and I went to my friend's house in Farnworth to collect the bike.

It was a B.S.A. flat tank and all hand-controlled. Although I could drive almost any car by then, I had to ask my friend to give me a demonstration on how to drive my new toy home. It wasn't taxed or insured but I drove it home via Little Lever, Ainsworth, Tottington and Affetside to home. This 'round trip' was so I could avoid driving through Bradshaw, where the local policeman knew me.

Learning to shoot

ALSO ABOUT THIS time my Grandad taught me how to carry, hold and handle a gun. As gamekeepers at that period, we had three guns in the house, and though Our Wilf could take a gun out, Grandad (quite rightly) would not allow me out on my own. He always said, "I'll teach thee, and when I think thy art ready, thee con go out."

Soon it was time for my first proper lesson but when Grandad asked me if I would like to go with him to 'get a bit of ferret meat' what I didn't expect was a very intensive lesson in the use of firearms.

My first 'target' was an old magpie's nest. Grandad told me how to load, put off the safety catch, put the gun to shoulder, aim and fire, left barrel and then right. My first attempt appeared to be a good shot except that the kick of the 12-bore nearly knocked me onto my backside and I thought I had damaged my shoulder.

Grandad's only comment was, "Thee'll learn."

I thought that that was the end of my day's lesson, but no. After I had emptied the gun, he started off towards the house saying, "Come on, we'll see how thee can shoot!"

Going into the quarry near the house, he produced two squares of paper about two foot square. Wedged on the rock face about six feet apart he measured out quite a distance then said, "now stand 'ere an' load up. Don't put t'catch (safety) off 'til I tell thee."

When I had loaded he said, "Now then, when I say shoot, thee'll put safety catch off, gun to thy shoulder, shoot at that paper on thy right wi' t'left barrel, then swing to that 'un on thy left wi' right barrel."

I did as ordered and then he said, "Empty thy gun an we'll see what sort of a shot thee'll make."

A good study of the targets seemed to satisfy him and eventually he said, "Aye, thee'll do. Let's go an' get some tea."

I must have satisfied him because both Grandad and Our Wilf would let me shoot occasionally and then came the day, quite some time later, when I was allowed out with the gun on my own. On that day I was a mere 12 years of age, but before I went out Grandad gave me a vital word of wisdom, albeit in his crude, succinct style. "Always stand behind a shooter and in front of a shitter."

The year 1927 came to an end but, if I remember correctly, not before we had a terrific storm. The brook was in full flood and was so high that water was sweeping over the footbridge. While we was watching the torrent, a large tree came floating down and bashed straight into the bridge. Away went the bridge and the tree continued its journey to possibly cause further damage nearer the village. We put out storm lamps to warn anyone who may come along, as the footbridge was part of the public footpath and was regularly used by the locals.

The following morning I went to school but a policeman stopped us all from going in. The school had been flooded to a considerable depth and a very thick layer of mud left over everything and the powers that be were afraid of typhoid breaking out.

What had influenced their decision further was that the floodwater had ripped through the graveyard next to the school and disturbed lots of graves and some coffins had burst open. For weeks afterwards bodies and broken coffins were being brought back to be re-interred. One local wag was heard to remark, "Ah bet they all thowt it wor resurrection day!"

School lessons resumed a few days later, but not in the school. Some rooms over the top of the local baker's shop were allotted to the senior classes, and somewhere else for the juniors. It was months before we finally got back into school and because we could take days off, and discipline was a little more relaxed, we were sorry when we finally did get back to the normal school.

Sometimes a few of us stayed at school for our dinner (lunch) and afterwards, if the weather was fine, we would play football, but if the weather was unfit, we tried to amuse ourselves in the 'big room' (assembly room).

On one rainy day one of the boys found the Head's canes. It was seldom the head used the cane but on occasion he did not "spare the rod' and this particular boy had occasion to remember the head's ability from a recent incident. So the boy stood, with the three canes in his hand, then a 'brilliant' idea came to him. First, he asked if anyone had a razor blade and, strangely enough, one of the boys produced one. So two of us held the canes whist the other boy cut the canes half way through. Unless one looked very carefully, those cuts ware not noticeable.

A few days later came the test. One of the boys had qualified for the use of the cane and the headmaster followed the time honoured routine, opened the cupboard door, selected a cane, and bent it three or four times before use. Of course, the cane broke, and so did the next, and then the next. Examination of the canes did not please the headmaster and he quite rightly asked those responsible to step out and own up. Of course, no one was that foolish.

But the head was not to be beaten (pardon the pun) and the following morning he declared that until the culprits owned up, all games were to be cancelled. This was very serious, because that very afternoon we had a very important football match with another school, so the three of us owned up.

The head instructed us to replace the canes with three more. Near the school was a shop that sold wheat, corn, etc, and also gardening items such as canes. When we asked the owner, who knew all three of us, if we could have three canes and pay for them later (threepence each), he roared with laughter and said that we could have them for free, because we would be the first to try them anyway, and he was quite right. But we did get our football match!

The farmer who delivered our morning milk would sometimes wait for me at dinnertime and give me a shilling to take the horse and milk float back to the farm. The number of times he would say, "See t' Tommy (the horse) and tell t'missus I've some business on."

His 'business' was the local conservative club (strangely enough for the area and the time) and the day after I turned 18 he took me to the club and made me a member, the first licensed premises I belonged to.

I would take the horse and float back to the farm, see to Tommy, and then run for all I was worth back to school. I was always late and I always got 'one on each hand' but for a shilling it was well worth it!

Over the Xmas and New Year period we always seemed to have a lot of visitors. How Grandma and my Mum coped with all the cooking, etc, I don't know. Aunt Sara helped also, but there always seemed to be a lot more to do, even though a lot seemed already to have been done.

Apart from Gran's elderberry wine there was always lots to drink. Xmas and New Year's morning Grandad was always up first and as everyone came to the living room he would give them a glass of rum, whisky, port or sherry, depending on what was chosen.

Gran's elderberry wine was always strong and popular, the reason being when Grandma was making it and wasn't looking, Grandad would empty a bottle of whisky, rum or brandy into the brew and say to me, "Don't tell thi gran!"

The number of times I've seen him sit in his chair, drink a pint of 'fortified' elderberry wine, then take his pot to the kitchen time and time again during the evening, until he was very, very, drunk. But no matter how much he had drunk, at 10.15 pm exactly he would take his pocket watch out from his waistcoat pocket, carefully wind it up, and then announce "Well, time we were up them stairs..." and to my gran, "come on lass, let's 'ave thee", and off they would go to bed.

One night I asked him how he got to know Gran. For quite a time he just sat looking at his pint of wine. I was beginning to think I had said a bit too much but then, after much thought, he related the following.

"Well, I worked at t'pit near by a farm thy Gran's folk had. When I started to meet her, her father found out and tried to stop us, but by time he found out it wur too bloody late, I'd copped her."

I must have been a bit naive at that time because it took me quite a bit of thought to figure out what he meant by 'copped her'!

For a long time we had a big white part-Persian cat. We had several cats but only two, Snowy and Ginger, were 'house cats'. I used to feed the other cats at various places, but the two house cats were fed in the house.

Owd Harry's was the general venue for the local farmers and others and if their womenfolk went with them, such as Gran with Grandad, the men would go into the tap-room whilst the women went into the 'best room' or 'parlour'.

When Gran and Grandad went to Owd Harry's for a drink the white cat would follow them up the fields and sit on a wall near the pub until they came out, then it would walk just in front of them all the way, down along the narrow path that led over the top of the quarry to home. I think that cat must have thought it was a lap dog!

❖ ❖ ❖

~ CHAPTER 3 ~

Growing Up ~ 1930-39

WHEN I WAS FOURTEEN, GRANDAD sent me out on my first solo walling job, as part of his gamekeeper's responsibilities. The routine was always the same. Report to the farmer, note the time, do the necessary work, then get the farmer to sign for the time spent and that the work was satisfactory. These 'worksheets' Grandad took to the Hunt Secretary when he went for his monthly pay cheque.

The 'walling money' Grandad would give to Our Wilf and me, according to the amount of walling we had done. That money I saved up and it paid for my holidays, year after year until I was twenty-three. Most of those holidays were spent on the Isle of Man.

At the end of the hunting season Grandad was also responsible for the allocation of 'railing tickets'. Each farmer was allowed 'railing wood' according to the acreage. The farmer would go to the local timber yard to collect the wood, all of which was stamped with the hunt's initials.

The farmers used to 'tip' us when we gave them their tickets, anything from 6d (6 old pence, 2.5p) to 5 shillings (25p). We didn't see much new fencing going up after the issue of railing wood, but it was amazing the number of new cotes and buildings that went up around the farms.

While Our Jim was living with us in The Jumbles, before he moved into his house at Affetside, he had gone out one night in his motorised chair. When the time got to well past the usual time for his return home we were all naturally becoming very concerned. We all kept going to the gate and looking up the road and on one occasion Grandad and I walked up the track to the main road (approximately half a mile each way).

Eventually, as we were coming back down the lane, we heard a crunch of wheels and saw a storm lamp swinging in the distance behind us. Then we heard Our Jim coaxing the horse that was yoked up to a flat cart and on the cart was Jim's chair.

Grandad said, "What the bloody hell's goin on?" then Gran said, "Oh my God!"

Our Jim swung himself down off the cart and somehow got his chair down with our help. We all stood there, expecting an explanation, but all Jim offered, grinning, was, "I got it cheap."

After unyoking the horse, I led it round to where there was a spare shed near to where Gran had her brooder. I fed it, watered it and as well as I could, groomed it. The poor thing did seem grateful and gave a contented whinny as I took the lamp and made fast the door.

In what seemed a very short time Our Jim had organized himself a sales/delivery round selling pots, pans, hardware and a tank with a tap on which he filled with paraffin. He would go round to the farms, big houses and local villages, where he established quite a trade.

My main job was to see to the welfare of the horse, which I was happy to do. Eventually he sold the business when he moved to Affetside and I was very sad to see this business go, as I had become quite fond the horse.

Entertainment

FOR MUSICAL ENTERTAINMENT there was a gramophone with a huge speaker, which my Gran used to almost put her head in to hear, whilst I had the very latest portable record player.

Of course, Grandad had to boast about this latest musical marvel and wanted to take it up to Owd Harry's, along with records, so they could all listen to it. Of course, Grandad couldn't read the labels on the records, so I was delegated to pick and play them (was this the first pub disco?).

So off we went, with a selection of marches, some Great War songs and stories, and two records, parts 1, 2, 3 and 4 of the landing of the British troops in France. Some of the older customers, and some not so old, would lean on their sticks, sat like they had had a spell cast on them, and every so often they would nod their head, and say, "Aye, it wur jus' like that..."

All in all, I think my gramophone recital was a resounding success.

The family, as a whole, were quite musical. Grandad, our Jim and our Wilf could all play the concertina melodeon and Grandad was quite good with the mouth-organ. Grandad tried to teach me the mouth-organ but all I ever learned to play was what Grandad called 'The Queen' and I called 'The King' but was in fact the National Anthem.

Our Wilf, my mother and Aunt Sara were all good singers but I was the odd one out. Even at school, whenever it was music or singing lesson, I was banished to the small science room to clean the equipment. I didn't mind this in the least, because the music/singing lesson was always the last lesson in the afternoon, so I could always slide off home early and not be missed.

I don't quite remember how old I was at the time when our Jim bought an organ which was worked by two pedals which had to be pushed down alternately to make the organ play. Of course, our Jim couldn't work the pedals, even with his false legs, and since I was the smallest in the house I was nominated pedal pusher.

I would kneel between our Jim's legs and push on those pedals until my arms felt like they were dropping off, whilst our Jim sat there, getting all sorts of noises out of that damned organ. How I hated that 'instrument of torture'.

Another instrument of entertainment which I looked upon as a form of torture was that forerunner of today's largest industry, the crystal set (radio).

I dare not speak, sneeze, walk across the floor or even breathe when they were trying to hear some elusive voice transmitted across the airways (at times it sounded like it was in some dim and distant galaxy!) and outside the house there was enough aerial wire to equip a large transmitting station. Eventually, when the 'cat's whisker' era ended, we got a more reliable radio with a clearer signal.

Pigeons

When Grandad was on his rounds checking the land, he would meet many people and stop and chat, and sometimes he would come home with the results of those chats. If he had been talking to a certain butcher, who was also a farmer, which always seemed to be on a Friday or Saturday, he would arrive home well loaded with some of the butchers produce, no doubt for some favour or trade.

On one particular day he came home carrying a large basket. At first I thought it was domestic fowl of some description, hens or geese, but the noises from the basket could only be made by pigeons. He put the basket down saying,

"Come on Pea, these are thy birds, so give us a 'ond t' make a loft fur 'em."

In a remarkably short time a very efficient loft was constructed, complete with 'bob wires', a simple device that allowed a pigeon to enter the loft but when the wires were set, the bird could not go out again.

To get the birds to settle in their new home, the bob wires came into use for a varying length of time. The pigeons he brought was not the usual racing pigeons or homers, but of two different types, known as 'tipplers' and 'tumblers'.

A tumbler will fly in circles to a very great height and then tumble down to within two or three feet of its starting point. A tippler will fly round with a group of other pigeons and 'tipple' over two or three times then catch up with the other birds.

In the quarry near the house, quite a number of rock pigeons had settled and they used to come down and feed with my pigeons. They were very fast flyers and the only pigeons that could match them for speed were the tipplers.

Watching them one day I got what I thought was a brilliant idea. I suggested to Grandad that if we could get a rock pigeon to mate with a tippler, and then mate the young once again with a rock pigeon, I would have a breed of racers that would beat anything going. I would register them at the pigeon club and could make quite a nice earner out of them.

"But," I said to Grandad, "the problem is catching them rock pigeons."

Grandad studied for a minute or two.

"Aye lad, its wurth a try, we'll get one or two o' them owt o'quarry t'neet."

Although I was only twelve at the time, Grandad had already instructed me in many of his poaching skills, but how he was going to take wild pigeons alive out of a rock face had me beat, though I never doubted he would find a way.

At dusk we watched the rock pigeons go in to roost then Grandad said,

"Come Pea, we'll get our gear ready. By time we've done that, them birds'll be settled."

Our 'gear' consisted of a net, known has a 'fly-net' and several tin cans, which we carried to the grass surrounding the top of the quarry. We tied the tin cans to the bottom of the net and then slowly and carefully we lowered the net down the quarry face, holding the net out with a stick in one hand and the cord that ran through the top of the net in the other. Eventually, we had all the net out.

Then Grandad gave a tug on the cord and we pulled the net into the rock face, making the tins bang on the rock. This startled the pigeons, which naturally flew out of their roosts right into the net. Quickly we hauled up the net and had caught five rock pigeons.

We checked that they were unhurt and carefully placed them in the basket we had brought with us. Then we took them home, put them in the loft with the other birds and I hoped that

Nature would soon take its course and produce a hybrid racing pigeon for me.

Every day I put food and water in the loft for them but although they happily ate the food they did not bother with the other pigeons and just sat near the bob wires, looking miserable. Eventually, after about three weeks, Grandad told me to lift the bob wires and let them go free. They must have told their friends about the free food because soon others came down to eat with my pigeons. Reluctantly, I gave up on the idea of breeding a super racer.

Fishing

I USED TO also do a lot of fishing. At first my equipment was what every little boy at that time used to go fishing with, a piece of elderberry bush for a rod, cotton for a line and a bent pin for a hook. Then our Jim started my graduation by giving me a 'real rod' with a reel and a line with two hooks on, and a proper float.

I was very proud of that equipment and used it for years, even though I eventually acquired more sophisticated tackle for fly fishing and pike fishing.

Among the many things Grandad taught me was how to snare trout or pike. Not many believed me when I said that I could do this, but it is true. He also taught me how make different types of lures for different methods of fishing.

Some of the waters I fished were private so I used to go just before dawn and would be leaving before the owners was out of bed. Although I fished private waters, Grandad never said anything, but on no account was I allowed to fish the Colonel's private trout lodge.

One morning I went to a stretch of water that lay between Harwood and Ainsworth. I left my bike just over the hedge, handy for a quick get-away if required. The water was noted for big perch and on this particular morning, in a very short time, I had caught enough to make a meal for the family. So I decided to pack up and go home for breakfast.

I was reeling in when suddenly there was a terrific tug on the line. I knew I had a good size fish and I also knew it was not a perch, I could tell by the way it fought. After a struggle I managed to land the fish, a good size trout, the first I had ever caught and I was so proud of it.

When I got home Grannie and Grandad had just got up. He asked me where I had been and what had I caught. Proudly, I put the perch on one plate and the trout on another. He looked at the trout and said,

"Ah've thowt I'd towd thi' not t'feesh them Lodges, now do'nt let mi ha't'tell thi' agen."

"But ah'ven't fished Lodges, ah went t'that place up Harwood."

"Ah don't want none o' thi' bloody lies! Ah feeshed that wather o'er forty year, an' ne'er copt owt theer. Nah that's a end on it, lets 'ear no more abeawt it."

I decided that quietness was the best policy, but I still felt disappointed that he didn't believe me, and the catching of that trout lost its glory.

We used many types of lure or bait and a strong favourite was wasp grub. I earned quite a bit of pocket money selling the wasp 'cakes' and it was worth the occasional sting. If Grandad was in charge of operations in the taking of the wasp nest, I never ceased to wonder at the casual way he would get the 'cakes out of the nest.

Wasps would be buzzing round him, crawling on the back of his hands and if one stung him he would knock them off his hand saying, "Gerroff y'little buggers, gerrof!"

Stings never seemed to affect him so much.

Grandad's usual method to get the wasp cakes was to cut a gun cartridge in two, take the powder out and put it into a toffee bag, tie the neck of the bag with about nine inches (we didn't have decimal in them days) of wire, leaving most of the wire sticking out. He then put the fuse through a piece of turf and placed the toffee bag into the hole the wasps were using, leaving the piece of turf covering the hole. He then lit the fuse, waited for small explosion, then quickly dug out the nest with a spade, grabbed it, put it quickly into a bag and beat hasty retreat.

One day our Wilf and I decided to take a wasp nest near the brook. Carefully and methodically we followed the drill, waited for the sound of the explosion, then went to work with the spade. We then got the shock of our lives. Instead of opening a nest full of non-combatant wasps, these wasps were very angry and ready to do battle. Two humans and a dog beat a very hasty retreat to the brook and tried to make like a fish until we had reached the opposite side. We soon realized the reason for the shambles. The nest itself was situated behind a very large stone and the small explosion had not touched it. We had merely invaded the privacy of a lot of angry wasps.

A few days later we did a careful survey and was surprised to see that the wasps had repaired whatever damage we had done and it was a case of business as usual, so we decided to leave them in peace.

After that episode we decided that there must be a more efficient method of stealing those wasp grubs and one day I had another of my brilliant ideas and discussed it with Wilf. In those days the most effective light for a bicycle was a carbide lamp. I was fitting up my lamp one day and checked that the gas was strong enough to produce a good light when ignited, when I got a whiff of the gas. I asked our Wilf if it was possible to use the gas to stupefy the wasps.

His answer was, "Let's gi'it a try Pea."

So, with an extra long piece of tube from the container, pushed through a sod just like Grandad's fuse, we had the perfect method of taking a wasp nest without the risk of angry wasps. This worked fine while Carbide lamps were still available.

A bit of a dust-up

When returning from a fishing trip one day with Our Wilf, on nearing the quarry near the house I could see some men fighting. My mother came up to me and said Grandad was involved.

"Come on Pea, grab that..." Wilf said, pointing to a stout fallen branch of a tree, "and use it!"

Obeying the command, I picked up the weapon and we went into the fray.

Following very early combat instructions and lessons from Grandad, Our Wilf and Jim I did not try to hit them on their heads but remembered a piece of wisdom given to me,

"Fotch 'em daewn t'bloody knees, then thee con put thi bloody boot in!" which I did.

Meanwhile, Wilf and Grandad dealt with them in the usual fashion and soon the assailants took flight.

Grandad turn to me and Wilf, but instead of words of thanks all he said was, "You took yer bloody time gerrin 'ere!"

Some time later, remarks were passed by some would-be poachers about the abilities of one Gamekeeper they called 'Cherry', who was quite a deterrent and another poacher joined in,

"Aye, but it's not just Cherry, it's 'is bloody army he 'as to 'elp him!"

Scouting

For quite a long time I was a member of the Scout movement and Bolton Lads Club. But when I finished at the Bolton Lads Club I thought I would join Bradshaw Bleach Works Club, but as I didn't work at Bradshaw Bleach Works there was some opposition to my membership. A friend suggested that, as I was a Scout, why didn't I join Bradshaw Scout troop, which used the club.

So I joined the Rover Scouts and enjoyed my time with them and became firm friends with a fellow Scout, Phil Daniels. We spent a lot of time together, fell walking in the Lake District and the Yorkshire Dales.

I would often take some of the younger Scouts on Nature Rambles and point out different bird and animal tracks and some of them became quite keen. Years later, after the war, I went in a local Conservative Club, as I approached the bar a smart well-built fellow stood at the bar said,

"Hello Percy, how is things?"

He could see I was trying to figure out who he was, he smiled and said, "Don't you remember me?"

"No, I am sorry, I can't place you," I replied.

I still couldn't place him, even when he told me his name.

"I was one of the scouts you used to take on the Nature Rambles. I used to really enjoy those and found your knowledge very impressive".

We had some visitors from the Scout Group HQ one time and I gave a talk on the local bird and animal life. The visitors were quite impressed and asked me to give a talk at the HQ, which I did. The result was that I was invited to give talks at various places and even got my name in the *Bolton Journal* a few times.

Starting Work

My busy life of learning, getting into scrapes and enjoying life in general went on until 1929, another 'milestone' year. I turned 14 in October and by November I had started work.

Through a mix-up with the headmaster, I left school before the end of term. The reason? Just to prove a point to myself, I took the scholarship class and passed for Canon Slade Grammar School (then a very good school and I believe it still is, having managed to avoid being turned comprehensive. Who said poor people were condemned by the 11 plus?). After passing this exam I saw no reason to continue schooling, so I didn't!

A day or two after I had turned 14, I went out one morning with Grandad on one of his rounds, which consisted of arranging wall repairs with two farmers for damage caused by the hunt.

About lunch-time we had got back to Owd Harry's. Facing the door was a stile to a path down to our house. Grandad made for the pub door and I made for the stile. He stopped, turned to me and said,

"Where art gooin? Dus't not want a drink?"

Quite surprised, I said I would, so into the tap-room we went. There were a few of the old boys having their usual and I sat in the exact place where I had sat to give the gramophone recital.

"Wa'rt 'avin?" Grandad asked.

Feeling brave I said I would have a shandy. Grandad looked at me as if he couldn't believe what he had heard.

"I'm not payin' for no bloody pop! Two pints Harry."

So Harry brought in two willow-pattern pint pots and filled them with ale out of a large jug. I had five pints that day and staggered down the road with Grandad at the side of me, grinning like a Cheshire cat.

Gran was stood at the gate, and when she saw me she was far from pleased. The resulting dialogue was short, sharp, and to the point. Gran raced up,

"Look at him! Where as't ad him?"

Grandad, still grinning, replied, "Owd Harry's."

"Thee wants some sense, getting t'lad in that state," Gran scolded.

"He's big enoof, he's owd enoof, he as t'larn sometime." Grandad reasoned.

That seemed to be then end of the discussion.

The next time I visited Owd Harry's I went with our Wilf a few days later. He said,

"Well, if t'owd chap con take thee in, I con, come on, I'll buy thee a pint."

So my drinking career officially began, at least as far as the family was concerned.

I had been working at the Bleachworks for three months when the headmaster saw my mother on Bradshaw Road and asked her how I was getting on at Grammar School. My mother was very surprised and became very angry when she learned what I had done.

I suppose I was a bit stupid, but I had got a job when jobs were hard to come by. In fact, I was never out of work from leaving school to retiring at the age of 65, and even then I continued working part time for a few years.

The job at the Bradshaw Bleachworks near Bolton had the added attraction of me knowing most of the lads through going to the Bolton Lads Club. Also the Bleacher, who was my boss, the under-bleacher, and his helper, all knew my Grandad very well, so I became known as 'Cherry'.

I have good memories of the one year I was there, I had a lot in common with them, and in our lunch hour we would play football, piggy and often we would wrap our hands in soft cloth and have boxing sessions. In fact, one lad who later joined the army became the regimental boxing champion.

But 'short time' became more frequent than full time, and although I had more time to enjoy my hobby of cycling in the Yorkshire Dales, one can have too much of a good thing, so one day I went to the local recruiting office to join the navy.

The officer there gave me a short test, which wasn't very hard, and I was given a form for my mother to sign, because I was only fifteen. But my mother refused to sign, not even when the rest of the family said it would be good for me. I must admit, I resented my mother's refusal for a very long time.

At fifteen I was competent in the handling of a gun. Grandad would give me four cartridges, saying,

"Go an'get a bit o' ferret meat."

This meant preferably a rabbit or two, instead of a bird. We would skin the rabbit and Gran would stretch the skin out and cure it with a mixture of alum and something else which she would not divulge to anyone.

When I was a little older I had two pairs of gauntlets lined with home-cured rabbit skin, which I used when I was out on the motorbike and they was both lovely and warm.

One day I was out near the lodges with dog and gun when I noticed two dogs running about exactly where I was hoping to find a rabbit or two. I was a bit annoyed about this and I soon recognized the dogs as belonging the Colonel at the Hall, but I did not know the girl who was with them, so I decided to investigate.

She told me she was a servant at the Hall and had only been there two days. I told her who I was and we was having a nice chat when it started to rain. I suggested we shelter in a small hut nearby, that the Waterman used to have his meals in. The hut would only hold the two of us, so I made the dogs sit outside and closed the door to stop the rain blowing in.

We were quite close together, sheltering in the small hut and getting more friendly, and I was just toying with the idea of seeing if what was said about servant girls was true when the door opened and Grandad stood there and I could tell he was not pleased with the situation.

"What the 'ell's gooin' on?" he asked.

"We're shelterin' from t'rain."

"What bloody rain? There's bin no rain fo' last half hour.' C'mon, lets be 'avin thi..."

A hurried goodbye was made to my new friend and I made for home with Grandad.

After a few minutes of walking in silence, he asked, "Did t'get any ferret meat?"

I displayed the one rabbit I had managed to get. He glanced at the rabbit and said,

"Thee knows, thee be bloody careful. If yon lass gets in lumber, she'll get sacked."

I must have been very green, because it was a long time before I worked that one out!

A Turning Point

WHEN I WAS sixteen I got work at a pit (Mosely Common) where I was to work for the next five years. Again, I met some good workmates and I did very well. Not only was the work very regular, but after a time I started to get overtime work of varying types. Over this period I had a variety of tasks, some 'on the top' and a few underground.

I was pleased with myself at securing a job, but Grandad wasn't.

"There's nowt in t'pit lad. There'll come a time when th'only lump o' coal they'll see'll be in a bloody museum!"

Very prophetic for the time (1931) and rather remarkable for a man who had only just learnt to write his name.

About the time I started at The Pit, our crystal set had become redundant. Grandad had encountered a man who had a wireless set for sale, so he detailed our Wilf and myself to go and collect it. This man lived in a caravan quite a way across the fields and when I saw what we had to carry back I realised why he had asked the two of us to collect his wireless. Besides the set itself, which wasn't small, there was a huge speaker, four 'wet' batteries, three 'dry' batteries and miles of different kinds of wire. Fortunately, we were both fit and strong, but by the time we had got the set home we felt we had earned a reviver, so we helped ourselves to Gran's home-made beer.

We then tried to get the wireless working. None of us had the faintest idea how to connect it up, so Our Wilf concluded that first we must have to set the aerial up. Of course, I was delegated for that honour, which meant I had to climb first one tree, then another, fastening a wire to the tallest branches, then climb onto the house roof and fasten the 'lead in'.

I must admit I was quite proud of that aerial arrangement; it would have done any transmitting station proud!

Then came the job of putting the wireless set together. First of all there were the correct wires to be connected to the correct terminals of the correct batteries. We connected the 'wet' battery first, then there were the plugs to a large 'dry' battery and then the plugs to a smaller battery called a 'grid bias'. Then we connected the aerial and finally the speaker.

Finally, we switched the set on but all we could hear was a very faint noise in the background, which could be anything.

None of us were very pleased with the end result of our labours and our Wilf soon lost interest and decided he would be better employed taking the dogs out with the gun.

Grandad sat there, smoking his pipe and quietly watching the proceedings with some mild amusement while Gran busied herself, muttering something about 'a waste of blasted money'.

I fiddled around with the wires (not having a clue what I was doing) and then I turned my attention to the speaker. Underneath the horn was a round thing, like a ridged wheel. I turned it and suddenly music bellowed out to my surprise and joy.

Grandad applauded my achievement with 'turn that bloody noise down!' It was so loud that Gran, who was quite was deaf, came out of the kitchen to see what the commotion was.

Later on in my radio studies I was to use that bottom half of the speaker in one or two experiments, that was to be my introduction to the 'moving coil', a very practical lesson in electro-magnetism, but of course I didn't know anything about it at the time.

Because of the result of my 'fiddling', I became the designated radio expert and from then on if the set didn't work to satisfaction, and I happened to be out, Grandad would say,

"Leave it till our Pea comes in, he'll fix it."

I have to admit that from that time on I took a great interest in radio and bought a few books to increase my knowledge, which gave me a good grounding for years later.

Gran became a firm radio fan and, instead of sitting with her head close to the horn of the gramophone, she did the same with the radio. She was fond of listening to someone call Henry Hall.

Shortly after that, she had no need to sit so close to it, having bought a wonderful contraption known as a battery powered hearing aid. There was a sort of harness she wore and this held a battery encased in a plastic holder and from this was a connector to a crude sort of microphone housed in another plastic holder, and from this were wires to a one earpiece headset. Not as sophisticated as today's hearing aids but it worked, and Gran could listen to Henry Hall in comfort.

Gamekeeper's Work

BEING GAMEKEEPERS AT that time, there were three guns in the house: a four-ten, a 12-bore (which the Colonel had given to Grandad) and finally there was Grandad's ancient muzzle-loader, which was almost 100 years old. To load it there was two leather pouches with copper measures on the end to measure out the amount of shot, powder and wad, which was rammed in with a ramrod that clipped under the gun when not in use.

Grandad was a marvellous shot with that gun, just as he was with the other guns, but he would not allow our Wilf or myself to use his muzzle loader, warning us that we would "likenly kill y'bloody sel's wi' that gun."

But despite that dire warning, one day our Wilf decided to try out 'that gun'. I don't know exactly what happened, because I was out with Grandad, but when we came home the gun was no longer usable and Our Wilf's face looked like he had stopped the charge of the Light Brigade.

I thought that Grandad would have lots of strong words for Our Wilf, but he just looked at what was left of the gun, then at our Wilf, and said, "I towd thee not to use that bloody gun! Thee'ad better get summat on thi face."

That was the end of the muzzle-loader, but it did not stop or deter Our Wilf's passion for guns. He was always more keen on shooting than I was.

By the time I was nineteen, Our Wilf and I were doing a lot of Grandad's work. This arrangement worked out well for all of us financially and it took some pressure off Grandad, who wasn't getting any younger. It was hard going for Grandad sometimes and he was grateful for the help.

About this time Grandad fell ill with shingles. He was very poorly for quite a long time, so our Wilf and I carried out all Grandad's gamekeeping duties between us. One of those duties was to accompany the Colonel as his loader and gun carrier when he went on a grouse shoot on the moors.

I went on the first one, but I would not go again and asked our Wilf to do the rest of the grouse season. I could stand sport shooting but that type of shooting I just could not take, to me it wasn't sport but murder, with beaters driving those poor birds onto the guns.

Although I did quite a bit of shooting, it was me pitting my wits against the bird or animal I was after and I would always eat what I had killed and kill for no other reason, but a grouse shoot was anything but sport.

The poor birds were driven over a line of guns to be slaughtered, this was not my idea of sport. The shooters was not hungry and they didn't even load their own guns. Each 'sportsman' had a servant behind him to carry the guns and ammunition and load and hand him the guns as he was firing.

Sportsmen indeed!

Shortly after my stint as the Colonel's gun loader, the Colonel came to the house while I was working on my motorbike. He asked me if I would do my Grandad's job and he would retire my Grandad. I was so furious I told the Colonel there was no way I would take my Grandad's job and if he did put anyone else in my Grandad's place Our Wilf and I would clear the whole district of every bit of game there was. The Colonel looked a bit surprised and then laughed and said,

"Very well, young Percy, it's your grandfather's job as long as he lives."

The Colonel kept his word. The last time I spoke to the Colonel was when I was serving in the RAF during the war, but when I eventually came home at the end of the war, they had both sadly passed on.

On the lodges there was always a good collection of wild ducks (mainly mallard) and we increased the number by a method of breeding known as the Euston System. By this system a pair of ducks which normally bred 8 to 10 ducklings would produce a further 8 to 10 from the same pair. This meant that instead of having 200 to 250 ducks in a season we had 400 to 500.

The method worked by feeding the ducks in a large trap all through the season, and about 40 yards from the trap was a small hut with the window facing the trap and a cord from the trap to the hut. Pull the cord and out came the pin holding the trap door open, keeping the trapped ducks in the safety of the trap until the shoot was over, generally 200 to 300 ducks were kept safe.

My job, after trapping the ducks, was to get the boat out and pick up the ducks the dogs couldn't retrieve, this was because the shoot was just before Xmas and there would be ice on the water which could be dangerous for the dogs. The colonel's usual guest for the shoot was a local mill owner, a Mr Ashworth.

One summer's day I was with our Wilf fishing in a nearby lodge and, as the afternoon wore on, the midges became very active. The irritation from the midges was becoming unbearable. I was being eaten alive by these pests and was sure they were queuing up to take their turn.

Our Wilf was sat a few yards away, smoking his Green and Gold (Woodbines) and the pests did not seem to be troubling him. I was twenty years of age but I had never given a thought to smoking, so he seemed quite surprised when I said, "Wilf, give me one of your fags."

"Thee what?" he asked.

"Fags... Gi'me a fag t'keep these damn midges off."

This he did and, after I had got the cigarette going and I was making clouds of smoke, I got a little peace from the midges. Just then Grandad came along. He stood for a minute or two, just looking and then said to me,

"Wot ar't dooin'?"

I seldom had trouble in understanding Grandad's forthright manner, he never said two words when one would do, but this time I had got his gist quite wrong when I answered him quite innocently,

"Fishin'. Why?"

"Naw," he said. "That bloody thing in thi' mouth."

"Oh that! I was beein' etten t'death, so ah' begged this off Oor Wilf."

He never said anything but took his tobacco pouch out of his pocket, cut it up, rolled it, and then filled his pipe. He always carried two pipes, just as I have always done since. He gave me the one he had filled along with a box of matches saying,

"Ere, if thea art beawnt smook, smook proper. That bloody thing'll kill thee. Our Wilf's too bloody stupid to tak' notice of 'is owd chap."

Many years later, some very clever people got well known, respected and paid a lot of money for coming to the same conclusion. They may have said it a bit more flamboyantly but Grandad had already come to the same conclusion in the 1930s!

One of the local big events was the Holcombe Hunt races. It was held at Harwood, the nearest pub-being the Nab Gate, so was called locally the Nab Gate races. The local papers described it has "The Mill Girls Ascot". It was also known as the Affetside Races, until the lady who owned the land at Affetside that they raced over, wanted more money each year, as the races became more popular.

One year she had a haystack built in front of one of the jumps and demanded money for the removal of it. Instead of being held to ransom, the Hunt moved the venue to Harwood, near the Nab Gate pub. As local gamekeepers, our part in the proceedings was to get up early and move off any hares on that ground, but this was compensated by the local pubs being open all day.

Working at The Pit

About this time, I started delivering coal as part of my duties at the Pit. I started these deliveries on Saturday mornings, when the regular driver was off work. These Saturday morning deliveries sometimes ran into the afternoon and covered areas such as Boothstown, Tyldesly, Walkden and Worsley.

I had a mate who knew the way around and we would fill the bags of coal from railway wagons and deliver just two bags at each address on the invoice slips and get the householder to sign for them.

We took no money for the coal, it was what was known as 'transitional coal' and was given to those out of work and on what was known as 'the transitional', a kind of extra dole.

Although most houses had coal sheds or bunkers, very few used them. At that time (1934) the coal had to be kept where nobody could steal it, so the coal went into the kitchen, in a cupboard, in a bottom drawer or even in the bath!

At the pit I was part of a core of workmates who were firm friends, varying in age from sixteen to the oldest who was over 30, and for five successive years we all went to the Isle of Man for our annual holiday. There were 23 of us and on the first night we would all pay for just one round, 23 pints. After that first night we would break up into small groups until the last night, and then it was 23 pints a round again.

I was still at the pit when I reached my twenty first birthday and decided to have a 'do'. Of course, all my mates from the pit had to come. We all met up in Bolton and put them on the right bus for Bradshaw, then I set off on my motorbike and waited for them at a local pub, where the party was being held, which was near a bus stop. A few of the invited locals and one or two of Granny's friends had gathered and when the locals saw these smart lads getting off the bus they could not believe they were all pit lads. I don't know what they expected but the landlord of the pub was relieved they were 'respectable' and not the rough miners he had expected.

When the party finished there was not a drink left in the pub, not even a soft drink and the landlord had to go to the brewery to get more supplies in before he could open the following morning. He remarked to my mother what a good crowd of lads they were, they had drunk the pub dry and yet there was no trouble of any sort and they all left quietly. Well... reasonably quietly!

Just after I turned twenty-one, my Grandad and I were rabbitting one night when my mother came to us in quite a state and told us that Grandma had been knocked down by a car and was in hospital.

We went to the hospital and I had quite a shock. Eventually she did come home, but she was bedridden until day she died. The morning Gran died I had to go to her two sisters, one at Hindley Green and one at Leigh. How I got round that morning on my motorbike, I don't know. I am not normally given to tears, but that morning I couldn't see the road.

From that day, my life changed once more.

Further Education

My interest in radio had more than increased and I was looking around how I could improve my knowledge when I saw an advert in the paper for Marconi Radio Operators for aircraft and merchant ships. I made enquiries and learned that one had to have a first class PMG (Post Master General) certificate, so I signed on at the Northern Counties Wireless School at Preston as an evening student. Traveling from Bradshaw to Preston during the evening to attend classes from seven to nine, three evenings a week, did not present a problem because I had my motorbike.

In 1937 I decided to take a local job at Bradshaw Bleach Works as a firebeater, so I could be home to spend more time on my studies, without travelling to Mosley Common and working shifts.

I soon learnt that there was more to being a radio operator than I expected, although I thought I had learned the Morse Code as a boy scout, I soon discovered I knew exactly nothing.

I had two textbooks, *The Admiralty Handbook* volumes 1 and 2, which covered such subjects as magnetism, electricity, radio waves, sound waves, valves and their components and many of the laws of Physics (Ohms Law, Lenz's Law, Faraday's Law, Kirchoff's Law, etc) which made me realize how much I had to learn, but I battled on with determination.

In addition to learning all this, I had to send and receive Morse Code, but as I had already learned some of this in the Scouts, it did not present too much of a problem.

So from 1937 to 1939 I attended college three nights a week. Again, I made some good friends and really enjoyed night school. In 1938 the threat of war was looming, so I told my mother that I intended to pick what I wanted to do and went to the local recruiting centre and volunteered as a reservist radio operator.

By that time I could send and receive Morse at 28 words per minute and I had been previously advised to buy the Postmaster's General Handbook for Wireless Operators, which contained essential information on sending and receiving messages to and from ships and aircraft and the various codes used.

One code I was advised to become familiar with was the 'Q' code, which gave me an advantage later when the Americans entered the war. A lot of RAF operators struggled with this to begin with, but I didn't know that at the time.

Life was going fairly smoothly when I had another upset. Grandad decided to re-marry. I wasn't too bothered, but my mother took a dim view of it and said she wasn't staying in the Jumbles cottage. I took no notice but when I came home from work one night Grandad was sat there all alone.

He put my food out for me and let me finish my meal, then he told me my mother had left and gone to live in the bungalow that Our Jim had built up Affetside. Our Jim had moved into a house on the main road, and my mother had rented the bungalow. Well, I was in a right quandary. Grandad said I was welcome to stay with him, but my place was really with my mother.

After thinking it over a while, I regretfully decided to go to live up Affetside with my mother. I had a quite a few pangs at leaving the Gamekeeper's cottage in the Jumbles, where I had happily spent most of my life. We had only lived up Affetside one winter and my mother decided that getting to work was a bit too much, so we moved into a house on School Hill. But, as things turned out, I did not live there very long.

As the dark clouds of war were gathering, I told my mother and Grandad that I was going to volunteer, so I could choose the service and the job rather than being conscripted.

The Navy, my first choice, told me I was in a reserved occupation (because I had put my main occupation as a collier), the Army told me they didn't want radio operators, so I tried the RAF. They asked my occupation, so remembering the Navy comments I told them I was a general labourer. That seemed to satisfy them, and a Sergeant gave me a Morse Code test, which I passed easily.

They then said that they would send for me and I thought that was the last I would hear from them.

❖ ❖ ❖

~ CHAPTER 4 ~

The War Begins ~ 1939-40

Basic Training

TWO WEEKS AFTER my visit to the RAF office (three days before war broke out) my mother and our Wilf came to the firehole (boiler stoking) where I was working and mother handed me a letter and said,

"A bloke on a motorbike in a blue uniform left this."

The R.A.F. had decided they needed me!

I took the spade I was using to stoke the boilers and wrote on it 'TO LET'. I then reported to the manager to tell him what had happened but he stated I was in a reserved occupation and he could claim me if I did not want to go. I told him to forget it. What would have Our Jim have thought of me if I had hid behind a reserved occupation after his experiences in the Great War?

The next two days were very hectic, sorting out my affairs before I had to report to Padgate (near Warrington). The last thing I had to do was to take my current motorbike back to the dealer. Ever since that first bike I had dealt with a reliable motorbike dealer and changed my bike every 12 months on a part-exchange system. The bike I had was a BSA Gold Star and I had only had it a couple of months. I told him I was going into the RAF, so he refunded me the full value and wished me all the best. So, along with many others, I joined the Armed Forces one day before war was declared.

Upon my arrival at Padgate on 1st September 1939 I was taken to a hut along with the other new recruits by a PT Corporal who was to be our guide and mentor whilst we were at Padgate. (Editor's Note : See Appendix 4 – RAF Padgate)

The second day after breakfast we were marched to a large hut and told to sit down. At one end of the hut was a bit of a stage on which was a table and three or four officers seated behind it. A senior officer then entered the hut and we were told to stand up. Apparently he was the C.O. (Commanding Officer) and after acknowledging the salutes he told us to sit down. Then he gave a talk about the Service and finished with,

"In a few moments you will be asked to take the oath and after you have done that you will be given the 'King's shilling' and a day's pay. Once you have done that, you will belong to the RAF and RAF Rule and Law. Remember, you are all volunteers, you are not conscripted, so you will have a few minutes to think it over, and if any of you wish to change your mind you can walk out and no one will stop you."

No-one walked out.

After the swearing-in ceremony, the Corporal tried to march us back to the billet (hut) and said,

"Right, you can do what you want until seven in the morning, then we will try to make airmen out of you. But remember this, you belong to the Air Force now, and we can do anything we want with you except give you a baby."

With that he left us to our thoughts. I often wondered if they gave the same speech to the WAAFs!

The following morning we were marched from one place to another and we finished up with a lot of gear including tunics which had been used in the Great War. In the afternoon we had all sorts of jabs and vaccinations and while all this was going on the sirens gave the first air raid warning I had ever heard, but it was just a practice!

We were then told we had free time until the following morning but if we went out we must not drink because of the inoculations we had received. I don't think any of us bothered to go out, we were still in too much of a daze!

The following morning, 3rd September 1939, war was declared and to the urgent calls of our Corporal, we assembled in front of the hut. Thinking back, what a sorry lot we must have looked, but at the time we thought we was the cat's whiskers and very proud of our status and commitment.

An amusing incident was that on this day we were square-bashing and the air raid siren was sounded. We stood looking at the drill corporal in charge of us, he looked at us and didn't know what to do.

Then he shouted, "Don't panic!" and ran like hell for the air raid shelter, followed by his lambs. It must have been a practice because by the time we reached the shelter the 'all clear' sounded.

With the guidance of the PTI Corporal we all started to change from the awkward shambling group into airmen, disciplined and coordinated which he did in just three weeks.

There was a lot of square bashing and a day was lost when he tried to teach us to 'form fours', but the next morning he told us to forget that because the policy was now to 'form threes'.

Then there was the passing out parade, our postings to different training establishments, pay, and a 48-hour pass. My posting was the first of the many cock-ups the Air Force, and indeed, any Service in a war situation, can make. I fully expected to go to a wireless school but instead I was sent to an air armaments school in Manby, Lincolnshire.

There I was taught all about guns, Vickers, Lewis and the .22mm canon and a few other things. We were taught how to align them, first on a range and then from a gun turret in an aircraft in a flying position, it amazed me how many gunners failed the turret test.

When I had finished that training, much to my surprise, I was sent to a radar station near Skegness. This was a very interesting posting as it was new, highly secret, technology, and this came as a total surprise. I wrote to my mother saying that I expected to be home for Xmas (as did many others at the time) but I hadn't taken the Air Force's designs on my time into consideration. The next letter she got was sent from France as part of the British Expeditionary Force.

We had only just settled in at Skegness when three of us were called up before the CO, who told us we were being posted to RAF Heston to form part of a new squadron to be sent to France. He said we had the proud distinction of being the first RAFVR squadron in France, I didn't realise at the time but we were now in 212 Squadron Photographic Reconnaissance Unit (PRU).[1]

B.E.F. France

WE FLEW FROM Heston aerodrome in Bristol Blenheims and our missions were performed with a French night bomber squadron:I was performing the role of Air Gunner. When we were not flying, we enjoyed traditional French food, which we all became very fond of, in fact we found it hard to re-adjust to English food on our eventual return to England.

We all experienced a strange feeling when we drove over the old battlefields of the Marne and saw some of the old trenches and even some straggly bits of barbed wire still lying around.

We stayed in a little village on the River Marne and the only way we could get a bath was to strip off, swim across the river with a piece of soap in our hand, rub ourselves all over with the soap, dive in and swim back quickly, as the water was usually very cold.

When we started this activity it was early spring and rather cold, but we got used to the low temperatures and by the end of March we really enjoyed the swim. One day, having taken our usual 'bath' earlier, I met a girl in the village and we got talking. She mentioned that I swam very well. I asked her how she knew, and she told me that she and her aunt had been watching us. I was most embarrassed as our 'baths' were always taken 'au naturelle'!

---

[1] *Editor's Note*: In early 1940 a detachment from the Photographic Development Unit was sent to France and was designated No. 212 Squadron on 10 February 1940. Operating the Spitfire and Blenheim, it flew strategic reconnaissance sorties over Germany until being evacuated to Britain following the fall of France. It was disbanded on 18th June.

Although she was the local farmer's daughter, she worked three days a week at her aunt's hairdressing salon in Paris. During April I was given a week's leave and I requested the orderly office to find me accommodation Paris. It was a good class hotel in the Place de la Concord. Even though it was wartime, the custom was still maintained to put ones shoes outside the room at night to be cleaned.

Because I had never been to Paris before, the girl arranged to meet me at the only place I could find with ease, the Eiffel Tower (little did I realize who would be passing under it a short time later). That week I saw a lot of Paris and my French improved a lot, although I still carried a French-English dictionary, which still became useful occasionally.

I was settling down to a routine and we were all getting used to the life when the German Forces decided to spoil our idyllic life. The first we knew about it was when we got blown out of bed one night from shell fire. We had heard some 'bumps' in the night but took no notice. That day we heard about Dunkirk and we got orders to pack up and move.

From that point on, no one seemed to know much about anything. We moved a short distance and took a temporary billet in a big chateau. The officer in charge asked if anyone knew anything about boilers and heating systems. I said I knew a little and he asked if I could get the heating system to work so we could all have a warm shower.

I had a good rummage around and traced the main pipes down to a small boiler. I asked the officer if I could have a couple of blokes to go in the wood with an axe and get plenty of firewood. While they were out collecting wood, I managed to make sure the water supply was sufficient for the boiler and started the fire with some loose wood I had found in the huge cellar where the boiler was situated.

To keep the fire going until the helpers came back with the wood, I knocked two doors down with a large felling axe. Once this wood was becoming exhausted, I took my axe to another door with large bolts studding it and a massive lock which defied all my efforts to open it.

I gave the door an almighty swing with the axe but the axe bounced back faster than I had hit it. Then I decided to have a look at what this door was guarding. I followed the wall round and came to a hole in the wall about two feet square, about four feet from the ground. I looked through the hole and saw lots of bottles covered in cobwebs.

I reached in and got the nearest bottle, knocked the top off and poured the contents into my mug and took a swig and immediately grabbed my head to stop it from taking off. I threw some on the fire and a huge flame shot up. When the lads came back with the wood, I told them about the free headaches and it wasn't long before we were all quite merry.

By now the boiler had reached satisfactory steam pressure, so I decided to put the steam through the heating system. this seemed OK, so I decided to go and get some more freebies. Unfortunately, I encountered the officer. I told him he could now use the shower but I must have slurred my words in telling him because he ordered me to report to the Sergeant and tell him I was under open arrest.

When I eventually found the Sergeant, he was aware of the party in the cellar and to cut a long story short that night the cellar was very much in demand and the drink, whatever it was, made everyone, including the officers, very happy. One person tried it in his petrol lighter, and it worked a treat. By the time the Germans arrived, I don't think they would have found much left. The next day we had to move.

We packed what we could into lorries and the officer in charge discovered that he was now in charge of more vehicles than he had drivers. I happened to be the nearest 'erk' to him and he asked me if I could drive. Without thinking about the consequences, I replied that I could, so he told me to get into the Dodge truck he was pointing at and follow the convoy. I had never seen a Dodge truck before, but we soon became acquainted.

The journey was a nightmare. The road was full of French (and probably other nationalities) refugees fleeing the approach of the German forces. There was just a solid stream of refugees which suffered periodic attacks from German Stuka dive bombers. When I saw these fearsome attacks, which were unopposed, I wasn't the only one who said, "God help England!"

So we ran and ran in what had become a country of scramble and chaos, and eventually came to an airstrip on the River Loire near Orleans. We destroyed our trucks using an Anti-Tank gun so the Germans could not use them, and awaited further orders.

We rested overnight but got no orders by the morning, so I decided to take a walk to the riverbank. I sat down on the bank and a very attractive girl came along, smiled, sat next to me and we struck up a conversation. Apparently she was a Spanish refugee from the civil war. She couldn't speak English and I couldn't speak Spanish, but we could both managed a sort of communication with our slight knowledge of French. We were getting along fine when the war intervened again in the shape of a corporal who told me that my plane had landed and was on the tarmac waiting to take off again and I had better get a move on.

The corporal and I ran back to the aircraft and just as I was just about to board the aircraft (a Lockheed Hudson) he gave me a letter and asked me to post it when I got back to England. I put the letter in my pocket and thought nothing more about it.

The French tried to intern us and stop us from taking off, saying the war was over, but we were having none of it. As we took off I 'warmed the guns up', which seemed to be enough to deter them from further attempts to make us guests of French/German hospitality.

Before we reached the English coastline we saw three Messerschmitt 109's but there was plenty of cloud cover and fortunately the skipper knew how to use it. Once we got over the sea I thought it may provide a softer landing if we got into trouble.

We flew over the Channel Islands and when we saw three Hurricanes going the opposite way to us we felt a little more relaxed. We crossed the Cornish Coast and eventually landed at Heston aerodrome, the place we had left six months before with such high hopes. It seemed like a lifetime ago.

Back in Blighty – 1940/41

WE CAME BACK, a squadron in name only. We had to abandon all our kit somewhere in France, we had no money and it seemed nobody wanted to know us. We were assigned civilian billets and a 48-hour pass, but I had no money and only the clothes I stood up in. I had a wash and shave, then went to see if I could get any money. I was told I would have to wait, but no time was specified.

But I did not want to wait. I had acquired a .38 automatic pistol in France (not Air Force issue) and I sold it, along with 50 rounds of ammunition, for £2 to the pilot who had 'saved' us. That was enough to get me to Bolton and to afford a couple of pints.

The following morning, I went to see Grandad. On my way I called in to the Bleachworks to see my friend, who was in charge of the Boiler House. He had written to me while I was in France. He told me to go to the office, as I was due some more wages, and this came in very handy.

When I got to Grandad's I discovered he had joined the Home Guard and he told me that Our Wilf was home on leave also. That was the first I knew he had joined up. He was in the RAF Balloon Section. So, after a visit to see Our Jim, I joined forces with Our Wilf and decided to stay the week, visiting all the local pubs, where we were invited to have a drink out of the 'soldier's box'.

I also caught up with the few friends who were still in 'civvy street'. By the way, I remembered that letter the corporal in

France gave me to post, and posted it when I got back to Bolton. It was a letter to his parents and the address was to a street in Haslingden.

When I went back to Heston, I was quite prepared to take my punishment for being AWOL (Absent Without Leave, a serious charge in wartime). I reported to the Station Warrant Officer and he asked me who I was. I told him and he asked me who I belonged to, and when I told him 212 Squadron he asked me if I had had BEF leave.

I said 'no', so he told me to go to the orderly room, get a pass for a week's leave, a rail warrant, ration cards, and more important – A WEEK'S PAY! I caught the same train back I had come down on, expecting to take my 'punishment', such was the confusion the Armed Forces were in at that time. I enjoyed another week's leave at home, much to the surprise of my family, and when I returned to Heston things were a bit more organized.

212 Squadron had been absorbed into a new Photo Reconnaissance Unit and was now 'in business' again. I reported to our own Logistics Flight Sergeant and he told me I would have to go into a civilian billet near the airfield. I reported to the address given to me in Cranford Lane and the lady showed me my room, which I would share with another airman.

Having sorted that out, I reported back to the airfield and was told that there was to be a clothing parade for 212 Squadron personnel. I got a complete new kit, because most of us had only what we stood up in. After clothing parade there came pay parade (again).

Someone said that there was a dance at a pub called the Red Lion in Hounslow (reputed to be where Dick Turpin selected his victims the night before which he robbed on Hounslow Heath, were the airport now stands!). It always amazed me that in any unit of the forces there is always someone who knows where to go and how to get there. So we arranged to meet our fellow airman, who was 'in the know' and would show us how to get to this 'Red Lion'.

The first thing we did, of course, was to sample the local beverage. Having calmed our thirst, myself and another airman decided to watch the girls on the dance floor. One girl attracted my attention. She was dancing with a soldier and I couldn't take my eyes off her. Soon I was hoping she wasn't 'with' that soldier. The dance ended and she went to join some other girls. I said to my mate,

"If I don't take that girl home tonight, then I'm taking no-one."

He said something about 'no chance' but by then I was going full steam ahead to ask that girl for a dance. The dance was the interval dance, so I asked her if I could buy her a drink. She said that she would have an orange, so I bought two orange drinks.

Her name was Joan and she lived nearby in Hounslow with her family. I spent the rest of the evening with her, drinking orange juice, hoping that I would make a good impression. My mates told me I had some pints on the bar but I never did bother about those pints.

I became crazy about this girl and met her every chance I could. Two days later I knew that I wanted to marry her and, much later, to my joy, she did agree to marry me.

During one of our evenings together, the Luftwaffe started their intensive bombing campaigns of London, but that did not stop Joan and I from going dancing. Sometimes the noise of anti-aircraft fire and bombs made the windows rattle and nearly made as much noise as the band, but we kept on dancing.

After I had taken Joan home, I would go back to my billet. The landlady, her husband and son were always in the 'Anderson' shelter at the bottom of the garden during these raids, and so was my room-mate, but I always went to bed.

In France we always said that if your name was on it you would get it no matter where you were. I went on the simple philosophy that if I had to go, at least I was going to be comfortable, and so I always had a good night's sleep.

The lady of the house thought the world of me. She was from Manchester and had the typical Lancashire hospitality. When

I returned to my digs one evening, and they were all down in the shelter, she had left a freshly-baked home-made cake on the kitchen table. I was very tempted to cut myself a piece, but resisted, as good food was scarce and I did not think it was the right thing to do.

The following morning I told the lady I had nearly robbed her of a piece of cake before I went to bed, but to my surprise she said I should have helped myself and in future she would always leave me a 'bit of supper' when I was out in the evenings.

I had a photograph of Joan next to my bed and when the lady asked me who it was, I said that it was the girl I hoped to marry and that she lived locally. The landlady seemed very pleased at that and for some reason took an even deeper interest in my comings and goings.

I was in the bedroom early one night when she asked me why I hadn't gone out. I told her that I was at that awkward point between pay days. She never said anything but a bit later her little boy came up to my room and said, "Mum has sent this, and you haven't to worry about paying her back." With that, he handed over a pound note.

The new PRU (Photo Reconnaissance Unit) was formed into three flights, one at Heston, one at St. Eval and one at Wick, and we rotated round every three months. When I was moved to Wick the winter months were coming on and in the far north of Scotland, in wartime, in winter, it was not much of a health resort.

A Spitfire had been reported to be down in the highlands and we took turns in going up in a Tiger Moth looking for it, but without results.

One day I was walking along the cliffs when I started to slide and could not stop myself from dropping into the sea. It is not to be recommended, bathing in the North Sea in the middle of winter!

My tour of duty at Wick finished and I happily returned to Heston. I wasn't there very long and the bombing raids were intensifying, so we were relocated to RAF Benson in Oxfordshire. Benson had not been bombed up to that time but that situation soon changed after we arrived. Within a week the Luftwaffe paid us a visit, just as they had done at Wick, and we moved once more.

But again there was the usual cock-up and I was sent to Blackpool, where the rookies started. I was put in charge of a civilian billet which was so bad I went to see the Billeting Officer who, in view of other complaints and after a short investigation, got the billet closed.

We were then moved into a billet where the great Stanley Mathews was in charge. He was a PT instructor and unsurprisingly his idea of PT was to play football. We had no complaints; he was a great bloke.

Shortly after that, I was finally put on course to finish the operative part of radio operator training (at last I could use my night school knowledge) and I was posted to Compton Basset. But before my posting I was due some leave, and I planned to take Joan home to Bolton.

She had never been 'North of Watford' before and the contrast between her middle-class home in Hounslow and the remoteness of the Gamekeeper's Cottage in the Jumbles came as quite a surprise to her, and not entirely what she would have termed 'pleasant'.

My New Posting

I FINISHED MY course at Compton Basset and waited impatiently for my next posting. When I had finished the course, I had to fill a form in stating my preference of posting. I just put 'anywhere' on my paper and I got quite a surprise when I discovered I was posted to Dover. I could not imagine what type of squadron could be at Dover, but I was soon to find out.

The train journey from London took hours. The train did a circular tour of the southern counties before we got near Dover and then we were held up frequently by shelling as the Germans in Calais were lobbing shells over the Straits of Dover.

The result was that the train arrived at 23.34 instead of 22.00. I had to then find the dockyard and a friendly policeman gave me directions. It was a good job he knew where I wanted to go because 'RAF Dover' was based in a big school overlooking the harbour, I would never have found it in the blackout.

I wandered into the school and saw an RAF Policeman. He took me to the duty Sergeant and I handed him my papers. He scrutinized these, especially my leave pass, as though he had discovered a rare gem. His face lit up and he said,

"You could be on a charge, you have overstayed your leave and you are adrift!"

I looked at him in amazement.

"What does it say on my pass?" I asked.

"It expires at 23.59 yesterday, it is now 00.20 today!" he announced.

I looked hard at him, controlling my anger. I was tired, I had had a rough journey and the last thing I wanted was some bumptious SP (Service Police) Sergeant giving me an earful.

"I have been on a 200-mile round trip of the Southern Counties courtesy of Southern Railways and the German Army. The train should have arrived at 22.00, it arrived at 23.45. If you have any problems with that, I suggest that you write out an official complaint to the Railway Authorities about their windy bloody train drivers who stopped the train because some bugger was trying to hit them with shells, and the German Army for sending them!"

I immediately regretted my outburst and thought I was in deeper trouble. He looked at me as if I was some strange animal and then just said,

"Come on, I'll show you where you can sleep. Breakfast at eight and I'll take you to the CO at nine."

I didn't bother to undress properly and within two minutes I was fast asleep.

The following morning at exactly 09.00 I was taken to the CO, who held the rank of Wing Commander and looked rather elderly for active service. He asked me about my service to date and then surprised me after he had looked at my papers by asking,

"Are you a good sailor?"

"Yes Sir," I replied.

"Do you *like* sailing?"

"Yes Sir," I lied. "I love the sea."

I didn't elaborate by telling him that the only sailing I had done was the crossing from Liverpool to the Isle of Man on the Steam Packet.

"Good... good! Take this to the orderly room, it's a bus pass to Ramsgate. When you get to Ramsgate report to the RAF base there, it is situated in the Naval Base. Good Luck!"

"Thank you sir," I said, then saluted and marched out.

I went to the Orderly Room where a cheerful WAAF gave me my bus pass, told me where to catch the bus and added that they were very regular. She was right and very shortly I was on the bus to Ramsgate.

I was even more confused. I had thought RAF Dover may be a bomber or fighter base, but what sort of RAF station was at Ramsgate? And why the questions about sailing, were they expecting me to be shot down in the Channel?

I soon arrived in Ramsgate and the bus conductor directed me to the Naval Base. On arrival I asked a Naval rating where the RAF Base was. He looked at me strangely and pointed up a metal stairway nearby and said,

"The RAF Orderly Room is up there," and continued on his merry way.

I went up the stairs, knocked and entered a small cosy room with two tables and about six chairs. At the first table near the doorway sat two airmen, one was a General Duties clerk and the other a Pay clerk. At the other table sat a Flight Sergeant and a Flight Lieutenant. This 'team' between them controlled the small bunch of RAF personnel at this 'RAF Station'.

These two gentlemen were known to all as 'Chiefy Grace' and 'Daddy Haines' respectively. The Flight sergeant looked at my papers and cheerfully announced, "Sir, this is the replacement Wireless Op."

The C.O. looked at my papers and in a friendly voice said, "Have you done any sailing?"

I was getting a bit fed up with this and, still confused, I replied, "A little sir."

I was starting to get worried as to why everyone was so concerned about my sailing skills. I was soon to find out. The General clerk was ordered to show me my bed space, where I was to eat and when I had stowed my kitbag, to take me to 120.

I was becoming more puzzled as to what 120 was and this was added to when I discovered my bed space was a hammock, slung and tied Navy-fashion. I dumped my kitbag underneath. I was shown where to eat, which was with the Navy, in fact most things were done Navy-style and we came under Navy Discipline for most things.

My guide then announced, "Now I will take you to 120."

He took me down to the harbour and along the harbour wall until we came to some boats tied up alongside each other. Pointing to one of these, he indicated, "That's yours, 120, the Wireless Operator onboard will put you wise."

Air Sea Rescue

HSL 120 WAS a High Speed Launch, one of four based at Ramsgate, and was used for Air Sea Rescue, which came under the control of the RAF and not the Navy. [Editor's Note: I couldn't find a picture of HSL 120 but found HSL 124]

I found the Wireless Operator and introduced myself. After a short demonstration he immediately started to gather all his things together, putting them in his kit bag. When he was satisfied he had got everything, he turned to me and said, "Right, it's all yours!"

"Where are you going?" I asked.

"Why man, I'm awa' hame," he replied in a Geordie accent.

"What, on leave?"

"Am I bloody 'ell! I've finished, oot of t'bloody RAF!"

"What? Compassionate grounds or something?"

"Awa no man, I'm a miner, an ahm going back to t'pit."

Strangely enough, some eighteen months later I was approached by a pin-stripe bowler hat type in the base office and he asked me if I wanted to go back to the mine. I told him I had left a reserve job AFTER I had left the pit and if I had wanted to stay in the pit, I wouldn't have left in the first place.

Then he said that I could be MADE to go back.

"Look," I said, "It's cost the RAF about £600 to train me, I have no desire to go back to the pit, or any other job while this war is on. You make me go back, if you can, but I can assure you that whoever employs me will think he's got a ghost working for him." Daddy Haines and Chiefy Grace couldn't hide their amusement and Bowler Hat made like he had a train to catch. Chiefy Grace then said, "Right, go back to your boat. I don't think you will be bothered again."

Anyway, after Geordie had left, I thought I had better make myself known to the remainder of the 'flight' or crew, whichever term was most appropriate I wasn't sure.

I found the skipper, a 'Flight Officer' and was introduced to the coxswain, a 'Flight Sergeant'. I returned to the radio and just had time to familiarize myself with the code book, the encoder/decoder and the essential call signs when I heard the motors start and away we went on my first 'shout'.

I was checking my set when a call came, giving the co-ordinates of a position. The standard procedure was that if there were air strikes or a bombing raid the rescue launches were placed in strategic positions under the flight path in the Channel, so if the crew had to ditch there was a good chance of them being quickly rescued.

While the boat was moving there was no problem, but after a while the engines were reduced to idle and we were at the mercy of the waves. I started to feel queasy and was sure the boat was going to turn over.

The lead to my headset was quite a long one, making it possible to leave the wireless cabin and go on deck and still listen in to the messages being received, this was also to enable the wireless operator to also send and receive Aldis Lamp messages. On this first trip the long lead was put to another use, I was able to be violently sick and still be on duty.

I lay on the deck and brought up all the food I had eaten during what seemed like my entire life. I soon realized why the CO had asked if I was a good sailor upon my arrival at Dover.

For the next three months I spent most of my time when waiting at RV (Rendezvous Point). stretched out on deck, headphones on, taking Morse Code and being sick at the same time. The first time this happened I will never forget the Coxswain, who was a nice bloke, offering me a bowl of soup, with a big piece of fat floating in it, which I refused.

The best piece of advice I received came from some fishermen I had become friendly with, who were still allowed to fish close inshore. When I told one of them about my 'weakness' they explained that swallowing the salt which dries on your lips when you are covered with spray, as often happens in small boats, causes sea sickness, and they suggested that I suck a piece of ship's biscuit, which will keep the mouth moist.

I followed his advice and ever after I had no more problems with 'mal-de-mer', I could even smoke my pipe and enjoy the coxswain's 'special soup'.

Eventually I got over the sea-sickness and started to enjoy the work and got on well with the small but tightly knit crew. I started to really enjoy the responsibility of being the eyes and ears of the launch. I say 'eyes' because we had RDF (radio direction finding) equipment as well as the radio equipment, wireless, and that RDF later saved the boat and crew.

On this first pickup, after we had been at the Rendezvous Point for a while, I received another message giving a position and the message 'Aircraft Circling'. This was the first of many such messages. I passed the message to the skipper and the engines fired up again.

After about 20 minutes they idled again and there was some movement on deck. I went out to see what all the activity was all about and saw two members of the crew helping an airman on board and two more of the crew pulling a rubber dinghy on board.

The coxswain said, "Here, you are Sparks, send this," and he gave me a slip of paper with the details of the pilot, which I had to encode and transmit.

I looked towards the nearby coastline, saw the harbour and houses and asked the coxswain, "Is that Dover?"

I thought he was joking when he said, "Is it 'ell! That's Calais – and we are getting the hell out of here!" And we did.

I think I may hold some sort of dubious record; within four hours of joining the fledgling Air Sea Rescue Service I had done my first 'pickup'.

Channel Rescues

I SERVED ON various boats and they all had the long 'trailing leads' and it wasn't just to admire the scenery. Whilst at Rendezvous Points they would stop engines and wait for orders. During this 'waiting' time the only person onboard doing any work was the wireless operator.

The naval base comprised the whole of the harbour area of Ramsgate. This meant two or three pubs and hotels closed completely and just one was kept open, which was run and manned by naval personnel for the sole use of those on the base.

We ate (messed) with the Navy and each launch crew had its own table (mess deck). For quite a while we slept naval fashion, i.e. we used hammocks, which were very comfortable (when one had mastered the art of slinging and getting into it).

The first evening I felt completely lost. I sat in the Mess whilst everyone else dashed about, those on duty getting ready to go on crew and those who weren't on duty (myself included) getting ready to go out and enjoy themselves, except me.

After my leave in Bolton, I had no money left. One of the other wireless operators saw me sat on my own and invited me out with them for a drink. After I had explained my financial situation, he said, "Don't worry about that, we have just been paid and I will stand a couple of drinks for you. My name is Barney Hughes by the way," and he vigorously pumped my hand.

"Come on, get ready and you can tell me all about yourself while we have a drink," he continued.

We had a very pleasant evening, which was the start of a very long and close friendship with Barney which lasted well after the war, but he did get me into some awkward situations at times.

One I'll never forget. He was Welsh/Irish, which way round I wasn't sure, but he spoke with a Welsh accent. He was tall, well-built and so good looking that all the girls were attracted to him.

One particular girl who was attracted to him had all the males in Ramsgate watering at the mouth. She was fairly tall, with natural blonde hair and her beauty was only matched by her figure. I never knew her name, but she was the daughter of a farmer who had a very large farm at Manston, therefore she had the nickname of 'The Manston Killer'.

Barney (I never knew if Barney was his real name or not, but everyone called him Barney) came and asked me if I would do him a favour and meet The Killer and make his excuse that he was on duty.

To tell the truth I didn't feel too happy about this, because I'd seen her in the company of officers who were plying her with expensive drinks and as I had just been paid I wanted my meagre earnings to last to the next payday. I pointed this out to Barney but he said I would be alright. So off I went to meet The Killer and off Barney went to meet a Wren he had taken a fancy to.

I met The Killer, made apologies for Barney and asked her if she would like a drink. She asked me what I was going to drink, to which I replied I was going to have a pint. She said that she would have a pint too. I was surprised at this, but I was more amazed when she insisted on paying her turn.

I asked her why she drank pint for pint with me and paid her turn, when I had seen her soak the officers. She laughed and said that if they were foolish enough to think they could impress her, then she would let them pay for the privilege. My opinion of the 'Killer' changed after that incident and although I was never in her company again, I wasn't taking any further chances and the only time I stood in for Barney after that was when he went to mass on Sunday mornings, this was possible because our boat was always 'stand off' when his was 'on duty'.

In the mornings, a naval Petty Officer would come round 'advising' everyone to 'rise and shine' and 'show a leg'. I never had the nerve to ask him if he went round the WRENs quarters with the same request!

The food was of a good standard and the portions were given out according to the number of crew of each craft. Each Naval and RAF crew went to the galley (kitchen) to collect the food according to the number on each 'mess deck' (table). This organization was according to naval tradition who, as mentioned, were in charge of the base.

All signals, radio transmissions (voice), or wireless transmissions (Morse Code) to and from all marine craft was controlled by naval installations on shore and operated to Naval Standards rather than RAF Standards. The main control centres for our base were at Portsmouth, Dover and Ramsgate, according to the area of operations and for the type of marine craft involved. For instance, I heard MTBs (Motor Torpedo Boats) working on our wavelength but never MLs (Motor Launches). The Navy expected, and insisted, on a very high standard of signalling, be it by lamp, flags, wireless transmission or radio transmission. To maintain this high standard, all signals personnel who were not out on operations between the hours of 8am and 9am had to take part in a daily exercise. It was no use missing the exercise, claiming to be at sea, because the immediate local control (Ramsgate, in our case) knew each tour of duty and where every boat was at any given time, night or day.

After every exercise, the chief naval Petty Officer for signals would come round and collect exercise papers for that morning. Then the naval signals officer would study them and if a paper didn't come up to standard, questions would be asked and these results would influence promotion.

Under RAF control, I passed my test by simply spelling out my name, and the speed of signalling was not looked upon as important. But when I started to work with the Navy, I found a big difference and it was a long time (as with most other RAF signallers), before the Navy was happy with my speed and accuracy.

This point was illustrated the first time a Naval signaller flagged me from his MTB. After the first letter I was completely lost. I sent 'IMI' (I missed it, repeat). Very slowly he sent INTRAF (are you an RAF signaller?). I sent an affirmative and VERY SLOWLY he resent the message so I could keep up with it. In time I improved and eventually I was accepted by the naval signallers, but it took time. This experience was explained by one Naval signaller. "We have a signaller for flags, one for the lamp and another for Wireless Transmissions, but you have to do the lot!" In the RAF, semaphore, although taught and part of the exams, was not given much priority (more than useless now with today's jet fighters!).

I soon got used to the pattern of "crash calls" and to save time I wrote out all the various ways the messages could be received so that when a call started, I only needed to check the heading.

With this method as soon as a message started to arrive, I would alert the skipper and we would be under way before the message was finished, thus saving vital time. I became known for being a good fast operator, which was an asset in the Air Sea Rescue service.

I had also worked out the various ways I could receive the favourite call, 'Return to Base'. But a near slip using this method actually turned out for the best and earned me great praise and resulted in one of our quickest pickups.

We had been lay on the Rendezvous Point for about four hours when the Wireless Set started chattering. I started to read the message and it started, "Return to...." so I shouted, "Back to Harbour Sir!"

So the engines fired up and we set off. I started to decode the remainder of the message but the last part did not match any of my 'standard messages'. The number of groups were correct but the decoded message confused me. I requested a repeat of the last group and the message read not 'Return to Ramsgate' but 'Return to Sandgate' which was a Rendezvous Buoy some miles up the Channel.

I quickly told the skipper I had received another message, not entirely a lie, and told him to go to Sandgate. A slight alteration to course was all that was needed and as soon as I had relayed the message I received a 'crash call'. I had only just handed this to the skipper when the lookout shouted, "Dinghy Ahead!"

It was our crash call. The fastest pickup recorded!

Everyone was congratulating each other, even the Pilot was commenting on the short time from giving the Mayday call to being picked up.

"I hadn't time to get my feet wet!"

I received a lot of praise for my 'efficient' wireless operation. I kept quiet about the almost disaster, realising that it was very fortunate that crash call came when it did and not when we were almost back at Ramsgate!

There had been a lot of criticism that various German Navy vessels were able to successfully 'dash through the Channel' without being attacked, so there had been an extra effort by Coastal Command to make their passage more difficult. This became apparent when we were lay on Rendezvous Point when an MTB nearby sent a signal 'attacking enemy'. I had barely written this message in my log when the same vessel sent another signal 'am sinking'!

Then the whole frequency seemed to go mad. MTBs seemed to be getting knocked out of commission like a coconut shy. No wonder, the most powerful warships in the German Navy were being attacked by MTBs!

Shortly after this, three torpedo carrying aircraft came over us at mast height. I think they were Swordfish. They waggled their wings as they flew over us and the cox expressed what we were all thinking when he said, "You poor sods...'

A few minutes later we got a crash call but when we got to the position all we could find was bits of aircraft wreckage. The leader was awarded the VC – posthumously.

On another pickup we rescued a Polish airman. As he was an Allied airman, from his dog tag I encoded his number, rank and name and his physical state, which happily was 'uninjured'. Some two or three months later we picked up a pilot, this time slightly injured, and when I encoded and sent the details from his dog tag I couldn't believe it was the same bloke.

When I had sent the message, I said to the Cox, "I bet they ask for a repeat".

Almost immediately, base asked for a repeat. Cox said, "How did you know?"

"When I sent the message a couple of months ago, they asked for a repeat because of his Polish name, look at his name, it's a bloody code on its own!"

We got one call very near the French coast. Sometimes, to help speed the pickup and to give the rescue launch protection, another aircraft would circle over the downed pilot/crew. I would then get the message 'aircraft circling', so instead of trying to find a small dinghy, which isn't easy in anything worse than a slight swell, we would just head for the circling aircraft.

On this occasion the aircraft circling was not the usual fighter but a Lancaster Bomber! So there was this Lancaster circling almost over the French Coast (this was before D-DAY) and it circled while we picked up the crew.

Recovery complete I flashed the aircraft with the Aldis Lamp "All OK TKS (thanks), the aircraft circled again and flashed "Going home". I replied "T (received) TKS".

Again the aircraft circled and flashed the same message, again I acknowledged. This happened another two times and we were still stationary very near the French Coast with the risk from the shore batteries and German MTBs.

The skipper came and asked what was going on, I told him they kept sending 'Going Home' and I kept acknowledging.

The skipper replied sternly, "Tell them to 'f#@k off', they're going to get us blown out of the water!"

"Plain English Sir?"

"Yes Sparks."

So I did ,and they replied "TKS" and off they f@#ked!

We fired up our powerful engines (twin Rolls Royce Merlins, the same engine that was in the Spitfire) and off we roared, just in time as the German batteries had woken up, presumably because they had noticed a Lancaster circling near the coast, but at full speed they could not get our range.

Marriage

THE TIME HAD come to get married. We decided not to wait any longer, as did a large number of couples during the war years. When she said 'yes' I spent an afternoon looking for a good wedding ring (I had already made a note of her ring size). I finally found what I thought was a suitable ring, and the following weekend I managed to get some time off and took the ring to see if Joan was pleased with it. She wasn't, so I had to take it back and get it changed. That sorted out, all I had to do was get time off to get married, which was no problem really. The lads from the base saw to it that I had a good send off and I had enough rum inside me to make sure I was warm enough till I got married. Three of the lads put me on the train and put their wedding present in my hands.

Now not having been married before, I was a bit hazy on the protocol of making things legal. I had told Joan I would put the banns up to be read out in the church in Ramsgate and she should do the same in Hounslow. Well, it seemed there had been a bit of a snag, so instead of getting things done the formal way, I applied for a Special Service Licence and we finally got married at Ealing Registry Office. Joan's sister Peggy and her husband-to-be, Sonny,[1] were witnesses and after the ceremony Joan and I made our way to Bolton. It was 23rd December 1941.

At the end of the week, I didn't feel like going back so soon, so I went to the local GP and told him I was due to go back from leave but I had a bad throat and would like a sick note to the effect I was unfit to travel. The doctor, who must have had many such requests, asked me how long I would like. I said that a week would do, so he gave me a note to that effect. I sent a telegram to base 'unfit to travel, request ration cards for further week.' That chore done, I went shopping with Joan.

The technical college in Bolton had been taken over by the RAF and wherever there was a service place where rookies were trained you would get that scourge of the Service, the Service Police (RAF SPs).

---

[1] *Editor's note*: Sonny was quite an interesting character. Before the war he was working for Shepperton Studios as a carpenter, working on film sets. During the war he seem to spend a lot of time building wooden aircraft and tank frames, which were used to help to deceive the Germans giving them misleading information about location of arms, especially prior to D-Day. After the war he continued to work for Shepperton studios as a set designer and worked on many major films. He told me his favourite was the musical 'Oliver'.

Joan had gone into a shop and I was stood outside when two SPs walked past. As they did, one nodded his head, indicating for me to go to them. I completely ignored them, so one came back to me and then the other.

The first said, "Why didn't you come when we told you to?"

I said, "Sorry, I didn't hear you."

The second one said, "You saw us nod our heads to you?"

I answered, "Yes I did. Bloody donkeys nod their heads, but I don't go to them!"

They seemed to be a bit annoyed with this remark, then one said, "You are on a charge and we will have to take you in."

I replied, "Look, this is my town and I wouldn't try to be too big if I were you."

"You can't talk to an NCO like that. How long have you been in the Service?"

"Three years as a VR," I answered.

"Do you know how long I've been in?" one said.

Quickly I answered, "Probably about three months."

With that, he tried to puff his chest out another inch and said, "I've been in fifteen years."

I looked at him in awe. "Blimey, fifteen years, and you're still a corporal SP, acting unpaid, unwanted. It doesn't speak much for your bloody intelligence, does it?"

This SP looked like he was going to explode.

He tried another tack. "No respirator, civilian-type shoes..."

I burst in.

"For Christ's sake get some service in! I'm on sick on leave and live in Bradshaw. This is the address of my home and the address of my base."

I took a letter from my pocket that Joan had sent me and took the letter out of the envelope and gave him the envelope, saying,

"That is my base, where we are allowed to wear civvy shoes. Send your charge through to them and they will laugh their socks off."

He took the envelope and looked at the address: 'HMS Fervant'.[1] He took it, saying, "You're quite a wise guy aren't you?"

"Too bloody wise for you, SPROG," I said. "My wife is here now, so long..."

And with that, I went off with Joan.

When I did eventually return to base, word had got round and the entire crew and most of the base, including the WRENs gave me a lot of stick for taking a week's leave to get married and another week 'sick'. It was very embarrassing.

Some weeks later, back at base, I was on second stand-by and was having a nice afternoon kip when the orderly room clerk came for me and said, "You, you're to come to the office at once, you're on a charge!"

The only serious crime that was possible to warrant a charge was to miss your boat on a call out and I hadn't done that, not that I could recall. The Commanding Officer, Dadddy Haines, was there and the Flight Sergeant (discipline), also a great bloke.

The C.O. started proceedings by saying, "Do you know of a place called, er... Bolton?"

"Yes sir, that is my home town, sir," I replied.

"Ah well, we have a charge sheet here. 'Using foul language' and other things we will ignore. What happened?"

I told him in detail of the encounter with the SPs and when I had finished I asked, "Could I ask who pressed this charge sir?"

The CO looked at the charge sheet. "An acting corporal so-and-so" (I forget the name) and read out his number.

From the number I said, "I wasn't far out when I said he'd been in the service three months."

The Flight Sergeant said, "Not far out sir, he's been in exactly fifteen weeks!"

---

[1] *Editor's note*: HMS Fervant was the shore storage facility used by the Navy in Ramsgate during World War II. It is widely believed that these tunnels and rooms alone are HMS Fervant, however much of Ramsgate harbour was used as the HMS Fervent shore base, with motor torpedo boats and motor gun boats carrying out operations against enemy naval forces in the Channel and North Sea.

The CO said, "I have to put something on this charge sheet to send back to Bolton, what do you think would look right Chiefy?"

The Flight Sargent grinned and said, "Oh, I think if you put 'seven days CB' that should make them happy."

The CO said, "Yes, I think that will do, OK Sparks, you can go, we just wanted to know about this place called Bolton and what happened."

That evening I went into a favourite pub to meet a friend and the first people I saw were the CO and 'Chiefy'. The CO bought me a drink and then I offered to buy one for them, but the CO bought me another and, turning to the Chief, said, "By the way Chiefy, just what does 'seven days CB' mean?"

The Flight Sargent grinned, "I haven't a clue Sir!"

The CO laughed. "No, neither have I, but it looked good on paper!"

As they both turned to go, the CO said, "Have a good night Sparks, but don't miss your call out."

I assured them that such a thing would not happen, and it didn't.

That base was a very happy base and as long as the boats were kept on top performance, "bull" was kept to the minimum.

The Dieppe Raid

WE WERE PUT on alert one evening and then told that only the crew of the duty boat needed to stay on the base. When we went into Ramsgate for a night out, we always had to give the telephone operator the name of the pub, or wherever else we were going, and if we moved from one place to another we had to ring in and tell him where we were. Obviously, we could only go where there was a phone.

This particular night, I went to a favourite pub with a friend where we were surprised to find it very busy, packed with aircrew from nearby RAF Manston. Among the airmen I noticed a wireless operator who had been at the Northern Counties

Wireless School when I was. I knew he had passed his PMG (Post Master General) Certificate and that he had got a boat. I asked him what he was doing in the RAF, because I had heard he had gone to sea with the Navy.

He said that, yes, he did go to sea but he took a dim view of the first boat he was on being sunk under him, so he thought it was safer in the RAF. The boat he was on was the SS Athenia.[1]

The following morning we put to sea long before daylight, all boats were ordered out. We got to the Rendezvous Point and for hours we lay there, there was very little traffic over the radio until just after dawn.

It started slowly but then as time went on the air traffic got busier and busier and as I was logging all this traffic it occurred to me that there was one hell of a battle going on and lots of aircraft and boats seemed to be involved.

Reading my log, a picture formed in my mind about noon that there must be a larger landing than usual and the RAF must be providing an 'air umbrella' and we were almost sitting under it.

Unfortunately, when RAF Air Sea Rescue boats were given certain positions, they stood a good chance of being attacked by enemy aircraft. Eventually, we were given a position but, having listened to all the radio traffic, I realized that it was outside the air umbrella. Fortunately, we didn't have to search long before we spotted the pilot in his dinghy.

We picked both up and I encoded all the particulars and had got about half way through this task when I heard the sound of machine gun fire and some commotion on deck, then my radio set blew up in front of me. I decided it was time to put on my tin hat and simply wrote in my log book, 'set u/s' (unserv-

[1] *Editor's Note*: SS Athenia was a steam turbine transatlantic passenger liner built in Glasgow, Scotland in 1923 for the Anchor-Donaldson Line, which later became the Donaldson Atlantic Line. She worked between the United Kingdom and the east coast of Canada until September 1939, when a torpedo from the German submarine U-30 sank her in the Western Approaches.

iceable) and told the coxswain, although we were already making for Ramsgate as fast as we could.

The pilot, though grateful for being picked up, looked up at the sky and said that he would rather take his chances up there than be on one of these boats. He then made the observation that we were 'sitting ducks'.

Back at Ramsgate, a new wireless set was quickly fitted and off we went again. As evening approached, we got another position, which was quite a way from our current position and by the time we arrived at our new position and started a square search, darkness was falling.

We continued to search in the dark until all hope was gone and we got the recall to base. But our 'day' had not finished yet… We had strayed into a minefield, so it was 'all hands on deck' to keep a sharp lookout. Stood next to me was another bloke from Lancashire and it was his first time out. He grabbed my arm and said, "See there… a bloody great mine wi' a leet on!"

I shouted to the skipper, 'Dinghy sir!' It was the pilot we had been looking for. Next to him was the huge mine which my fellow lookout had spotted. Very carefully, we sailed past the pilot's dinghy and then tried to drift back onto him. Three times we tried this until we could get close enough without endangering the boat, so the lads could get to the dinghy with a boathook and finally rescue the pilot.

The much-relieved pilot told us that just before we came along, two German E-Boats had passed him, so he had covered his light so he would not to be discovered. He had just hoped that we could find him.

But our long day/night was not quite over. When we were passing Dover we were challenged, shore to ship, with the Aldis Lamp. I answered the challenge with ship to shore communication, but they were not satisfied and asked me the number of the launch, where we were going and, lastly, what was the skipper's name. When we had answered all these questions, they seemed satisfied and wished us 'goodnight, proceed'.

Safely back to harbour, and still in time for a pint, one or two of the locals bought us a drink and told us they had been watching the boats come back in. The 'launch boys' were firm favourites with the locals. So ended our participation in the Dieppe raid![1]

Shortly after that the crew rosters changed and I was transferred to another boat with another skipper. We had been out on Rendezvous Point for quite a long time, it was dark and a heavy fog had come down when we got the recall.

The Skipper was a young officer and apparently not very experienced. First of all he must have got his navigation wrong because we ran onto a sandbank and we should have been nowhere near a sandbank. Then he couldn't quite work out where Ramsgate harbour was.

He said to me, "Sparks, ask for Ramsgate harbour lights to be put on."

To say I was surprised to get an order like this was to put it mildly. The Germans shelled the towns in the Dover Straits regularly and accurately enough without lighting up the town for them.

So I started to encode the message, making it as brief as possible. The skipper saw me start to encode it and told me to send it in plain English. I just couldn't believe what I was being told to do, surely all messages, on both sides, were being intercepted. I hesitated, trying to think of a nice way to tell the skipper he was quite out of order telling me to transmit such a message.

He must have noticed I wasn't happy about the order he had given me and he seemed to be getting angry and ordered me to send the message off at once, a 'direct order'.

Well, I was in a quandary. I had a direct order from an officer during wartime, so I sent the message. Immediately, the answer flashed back 'Request refused'.

---

[1] See Appendix 5. The Dieppe Raid.

I must admit I derived some satisfaction on showing the skipper the answer to that stupid signal. Eventually, with the help of a small naval vessel, we made it back to harbour. We never saw that skipper again.

The following morning the Naval Petty Office (Signals) told me to get my log book and go with him. He took me to the naval officer in charge of Signals, who examined my log book, studied it for a minute or so, and then said,

"Now... this stupid signal you sent last night. WHY did you send it?"

I explained that it was a direct order from an officer and if I had refused, I stood a good chance of facing a court martial.

The naval officer said that he understood my position and then he smiled and said, "Now, I will give you some advice which I want you to take note of and never forget. When you are at sea, YOU and YOU alone, are responsible for all messages to and from your vessel, do not forget, *you and you alone* must decide on the type of transmission. Now get back to your launch and I don't want to see any more stupid signals."

That was a lesson I was to remember and those words of wisdom from that naval officer proved to be quite correct.

Encounters with the enemy

It was soon back to business and we got a crash call out into the North Sea. When we sighted the dinghy we were surprised to see it contained three Germans, one badly injured, one slightly injured and the other uninjured. He was the last onboard and on boarding he stood at the stern of the boat and gave the Nazi salute, saying, "Heil Hitler!"

This did not go down well, as we had come all this way to rescue them and every pickup was potentially dangerous, so one of the deck hands had a long boat hook in his hands which had been used to grab the dinghy, he 'accidentally' swung round, catching the German off guard and he landed back in the North Sea. The deck hand grinned and said, "Reverse Sir?"

The skipper replied, "Much as I would like to, it would not go down well on the report."

So we roughly dragged a wet and much subdued young Nazi back onboard and he was pushed into the well deck, where he remained until we were nearly back at Ramsgate.

We then ordered him to remove all his wet clothes and put on survivors clothes, as his colleagues had already done, which were warm and dry. This was the usual procedure for all rescued crew, irrespective of nationality. The deck crew then examined the uniforms for 'souvenirs'.

If there was just a pilot in the dinghy, the deck hands would quickly judge the size of the unfortunate airman's boots. The deck hands were very astute at judging the size of flying boots, which were easy to sell, and anything else which could be salvaged and the nearest deck hand to the dinghy would go in the dinghy to assist.

On this particular pickup, once the deck hands had sorted out what they wanted, the remaining 'spoils' were divided between the rest of the crew. I retrieved some sort of flying badge, which was sewn onto a sleeve.

That evening, back in port, after delivering the Germans to the medics, some of us went for a drink. The following morning, I reported sick. I had a violent headache and generally felt rotten. The Naval medical officer had me rushed off to Ramsgate hospital and in a private ward where he visited me every day for ten days.

Then he asked me where my home was. I told him and how far it was, he then said I would have to go on ten days sick leave. I pointed out that I had only been back three weeks after my last leave but he repeated that I was to have ten days sick leave. I was to go to base, get money, ration cards and get the first train out.

I went to the orderly room and when I told Chiefy Grace he blew his top. I pointed out that it was not my idea, but the Navy medic's. Picking up the phone he raved, "I'll soon put a stop to that!"

I stood there, patiently waiting, smoking my pipe and listening to poor Chiefy.

"But he's just had... Yes Sir, but we can't... Yes, Yes Sir. Yes, Sir I will see to it at once, Sir. Bye."

He turned to me and said, "Go to the orderly room, get all you need, I'll have everything ready when you come back. You are not to take any kit with you. I'll have transport ready to take you to the station. Bloody Naval Medics, I just don't believe it!"

What he didn't believe, I was to later learn from our own launch medic when I returned from 'sick leave'. He told me that after I left, all the crew had to have a bath, the bathwater having had a strong injection of disinfectant which turned the water pink. All the spoils collected from the German crew were promptly burned.

In the harbour area, barred to all civilians without a pass, was a large public house, empty now with the access restrictions. So someone thought it a good idea for RAF Rescue personnel to billet there, except for dining (we were still under Naval rations). I don't know who thought that one up, but I reckon it was one of the brilliant ideas of those little gods of war, who got paid for thinking up ideas, most of which were soundly cursed by those unfortunates to whom they applied.

Anyway, we had only moved into this hotel about two weeks before the episode of the Germans and me going sick, resulting in my ten days extra leave. Whilst I was away the whole place was fumigated, including the clothes of the crew who had picked up the Germans.

I also learned that the clothes I went on sick leave in had already been fumigated while I was in hospital, then the rest was done and stored until I came back. All this was related to me by the crew medic.

It seemed that one of the Germans was a carrying a threat of the plague, VD or some other form of disaster to the human race, hence the big panic. So I never did find out exactly why I got extra leave through reporting sick with a headache!

Shortly after this incident we received a signal from the Channel Patrol that a parachute had been sighted and gave the position. We soon found the parachute and when it was pulled in there was a dead German in the harness. I don't know how long he had been in the water but when the parachute was pulled aboard we discovered that the harness was the only thing holding his body together. When he was laid on deck, a vast amount of sea life came wriggling, crawling and running out of him. We took his dog tags, wrapped him back up in his parachute, tied it up and committed him back to the sea.

Meanwhile, I sent a signal in plain English detailing his name, rank and number and that he was dead and buried at sea, knowing that it would be picked up by the German 'listening stations' and they could account for at least one more of their aircrew.

The deck crew got busy putting all the livestock back in the sea and scrubbed the deck to ensure it was hygienic. I have never eaten seafood since.

Help For Our Allies

ONE PICKUP IN the Channel I shall always remember was an American who was a member of the Eagle Squadron,[1] a squadron made up of American airmen who had volunteered for the RAF long before America entered the war.

I had never heard of the Eagle Squadron until we picked this American pilot up in the Channel. What was outstanding about this pickup was after we got the crash call we did a square search for two hours without success. Another rescue boat and a lifeboat joined in the search but could see no sign of a dinghy.

[1] *Editor's note*: The Eagle Squadrons were three fighter squadrons of the Royal Air Force (RAF) formed with volunteer pilots from the United States during the early days of World War II (circa 1940), prior to America's entry into the war in December 1941.

Then two Hurricanes of the Channel Patrol flew over at wave height and dropped a smoke float. The accuracy of the Hurricane pilots was remarkable because although a smoke float is small it could not have got nearer to him without hitting him, which would have been very uncomfortable for the poor airman.

We were then able to locate him and when we picked him up he explained that his dinghy had failed to inflate and his Mae West was useless. So for over two hours he had watched the boats going around him whilst he trod water and tried to attract our attention, but of course we were looking for a dinghy and of course it is very hard to see just a head in a choppy sea, and the noise of our engines drowned out his shouts for help.

Not long after this incident we received a call to a position in the North Sea but on reaching it we were not happy that we had been brought all this way to recover a barrage balloon! Still, we were looking forward to seeing some red faces when we showed the powers-that-be what we had 'rescued'.

If the weather was too bad for flying, the RAF administrators would inform the Naval authorities, who would in turn inform our base and the state of alert dropped to 'Stand Off', which meant we could go to bed.

To alert the crews for a call-out, a very shrill bell was rung and the system of ringing could send one or more boats out. You could not ignore the bell and not use the excuse of 'not hearing' it.

One night we had been in Stand Off and I was sleeping peacefully after having been out for a few drinks. On this night the bell rang at 0200 for the duty boat, which was my crew. We quickly dressed and ran to the launch.

The weather was atrocious, the rain was pelting down and looking out to sea the waves were mountainous. I thought to myself, 'surely no-one will be flying in this weather'. The sea wasn't rough, it was MURDEROUS! I was surprised that the radio equipment still worked. Anyway, we headed out into the North Sea.

We had been going about one hour when I received a message to cheer us up which advised that there was an MTB in the area. Base would contact the MTB and advise them of our presence, so we didn't start shooting at each other (our launches only carried a light gun on deck). A short while later our boat 'bumped' into something. I thought we must have hit the MTB. I went on deck and was amazed to see what we had 'bumped' into. We had not collided with anything but had come alongside a massive network of steel girders rising above us.

It was an anti-invasion fort, manned by marines, one of whom had developed appendicitis and had radioed for assistance. This thing towered above us, the sea was rough and I wondered how they were going to get a very sick man from 'up there' to 'down here'. This was in hand, however. He was tightly wrapped into a Neil Robinson stretcher, hooked onto a crane, hoisted over the edge and, after some manoeuvring, lowered onto our deck.

We quickly had him back to Ramsgate, where an ambulance was waiting for him as soon as we pulled alongside. Apparently, he made a full recovery and was soon back at the fort.

RAF Cranwell

BARNEY AND I were sent on a course to RAF College, Cranwell, which was, and still is, the elite RAF training establishment, mainly for officers. Some of the course content I had already covered at night school before the war, so I found it quite easy.

Whilst on the course I got friendly with some Canadians and went out with them nearly every night, resulting in me being on report for being late back and twice after I failed to report in, all of which was subsequently reported to the chief instructor, although I was not aware of this until later.

At the end of the course, we were given a test and at the end the test the examiner reviewed the questions and supplied the correct answers. Barney achieved 85% and I was given 80%, but when the chief instructor saw my marks he said, "Not Shipper-bottom! Not with his record! Three guard reports and twice failing to book in. There is something funny going on here. I'll give him a retest!"

So he did, and gave me exactly the same test I had just had done, but of course I now knew all the answers, including the 20% I had got wrong in the first test. At the end of the test the instructor looked very surprised and said, "It is just not done."

I enquired, "What is 'not done' Sir?", and he repeated, "It is just not done, the RAF just does not give 100%, I'll give you 95% but how have you managed it, with your record whilst you have been on this course, I will never know!'

I told him about my night school classes at the Northern Counties Wireless School, to which he remarked, "Well, that does explain a lot!"

The CO, my skipper and the coxswain were all pleased when our results came through officially, but during next few months things were to change dramatically.

First a signal came for me to go to an OTU (Operational Training Unit, aircrew). I was quite happy to go, but the C.O. talked me out of it, saying that I wouldn't be posted overseas if I stayed on Air Sea Rescue, as it was voluntary. That was the first time I had been aware that I had 'volunteered' for Air Sea Rescue, so I stayed on the boats. Then came the chance to go on a course for a commission (up to now I had achieved the rank of Flight Sergeant).

I definitely did not want *that*. The RAF was still very class conscious and the officer class was not the place for a gamekeeper's grandson from Bolton. More importantly, I couldn't afford it.

Barney took it, but he could afford it. After the war I met some of the old crew, including my skipper, and I enquired about Barney and learned that he finished up Chief Flying Control Officer at Heathrow.

Shortly after the offer of the commission, I received a telegram to tell me of the birth of my first son. The CO, skipper, coxswain and most of the lads wanted to know what sex the baby was and when I said 'it's a boy' the CO said I had better have a week's leave, but first the skipper said we must wet the baby's head, so out came the rum bottle (Navy Rum).

The father and mother of Phil Daniels, my friend from my scouting and fell walking days, consented to be godparents, because Phil always said he would be godfather to my child, but he was with the Anglo-Iranian oil company in Iran by then. He wrote to me all through the war and we met up after the war.

Whilst I was on 'paternal' leave I got a telegram with bad news.

'Leave extended further six weeks, overseas posting.'

I wondered where I was going.

At the end of my leave, I returned to my base at Ramsgate to collect my gear. The CO and the skipper both assured me that they were doing their best to keep me on their crew but I had a feeling that their efforts would be in vain because RAF wireless operators (as with most RAF operational crew) were becoming very scarce, so if I had been 'allocated' for somewhere I could not see how my CO could stop it.

I thanked them and said I would keep them posted and left to report back to Dover. The clerk in the orderly room at Dover said, "Ahh! so you're Shipperbottom, there has been quite a to-do about you what with phone calls and telegrams to Records. They even offered two wireless ops in your place, but a Records posting can't be overturned, so I think you'll be going to sunny climes."

How right he was.

'Our Wilf' on a shoot with Colonel Hardcastle.

Gamekeeper's cottage in winter.

Crowds gather after the Hulton Pit disaster of 1910.

Memorial to the miners who lost their lives in the disaster.

ASR colleagues at Ramsgate, (Author bottom row, 2nd from right).

My boat, HSL 120 in patrol in the Channel.

BEF, Coulommiers France, April 1940.

Locals at Seine-et-Marne, 1940.

HSL 120 on a call in the Channel, taken from wireless cabin.

Crew of HSL 120 making an ASR Channel pickup.

Our colleagues in HSL 149 making an ASR pickup in the Channel.

A closer shot of HSL 149 making an ASR pickup in the Channel.

Back in Ramsgate, completing logs.

Ready for the Far East.

Two ASR launches heading out into the Channel.

Calcutta – ASR Launch 226 in dry dock for repairs.

ASR Launch 226 moored at Chittagong.

ASR 226 sets off on anther crash call.

Hospital ship in the harbour at Chittagong.

HMS Fervent memorial plaque.

The RMS Sratheden.

Howrah Station, India.

The RMS Mooltan.

Just married.

Joan with baby Colin.

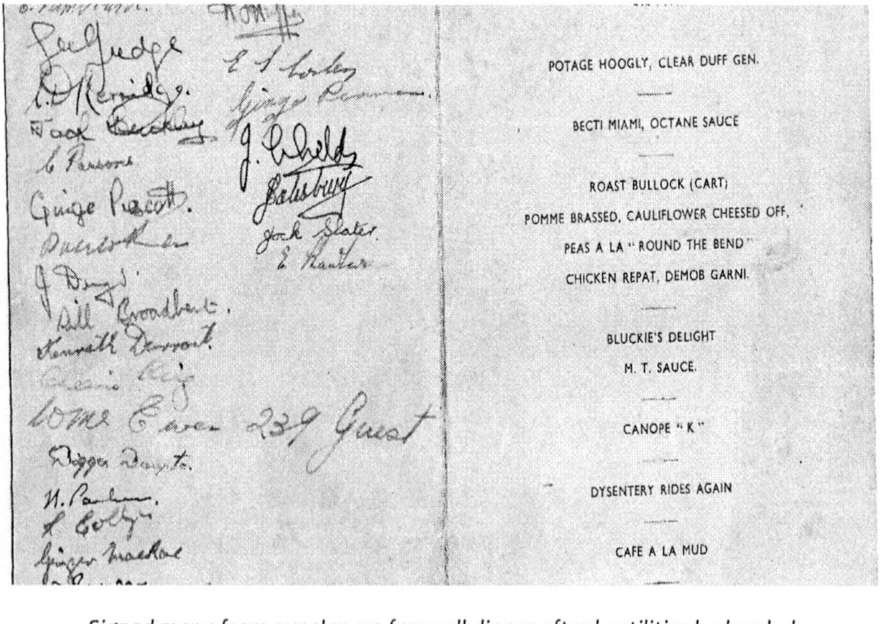

POTAGE HOOGLY, CLEAR DUFF GEN.

BECTI MIAMI, OCTANE SAUCE

ROAST BULLOCK (CART)

POMME BRASSED, CAULIFLOWER CHEESED OFF,

PEAS A LA "ROUND THE BEND"

CHICKEN REPAT, DEMOB GARNI.

BLUCKIE'S DELIGHT

M. T. SAUCE.

CANOPE "K"

DYSENTERY RIDES AGAIN

CAFE A LA MUD

Signed menu from our slap-up farewell dinner after hostilities had ended.

Territorial Army exercise, . 1964.

Newly demobbed and standing at the gate to Jumbles Cottage with Joan.

Percy's medals.

HSL 124 in the Channel.

~ CHAPTER 5 ~

Off to Sunnier Climes ~ Jan 1943

FIRST OF ALL, I WAS sent to West Kirby transit camp, where we were told that no-one was to leave the camp. As there was no booze on the camp, I and another Flight Sergeant decided we were not going to leave England without a farewell drink, so we broke camp.

It wasn't difficult and we quietly returned in the small hours. The following morning we were bunged into some lorries and transported to Liverpool, where we embarked on the P&o liner *Stratheden*. As we were boarding, the dock workers shouted, "Best of luck boys, there's plenty of bananas where you are going!"

So much for secret and confidential information!

The SS *Stratheden* was a luxury mail liner which had been requisitioned and converted to a troop carrier. Although the embarkation procedure seemed haphazard, the embarkation operation was remarkable. All the different trades were all together on the same Mess deck, so I got to know some of my fellow wireless operators.

By the time we were allocated our spaces and had a meal it was time to 'sling our hammocks' which had been issued. I had no problem with mine, after my time on the Air Sea Rescue craft, but it was amusing to see the positions some of those lads finished up in. How some of them managed to get some sleep was beyond me.

When we woke the following morning, we expected to be in the middle of the ocean, but when we peered out of the 'windows' (portholes), we were in an estuary in the company of a load of other ships. Whilst we were debating where we were, a Ginger haired lad exclaimed in a very Scottish accent, "Bloddy hell, were're at Gourock", pointing at some distant cottages. "That's my bloddy hame. I could bloddy swum it!"[1]

At lunch time an RAF officer came round, asking for wireless operators to make themselves known. When he got to our table he asked, "Has anyone here any experience of working with the Navy?"

"Yes sir, I have," I answered.

"What experience have you had?"

"Air Sea Rescue Sir, based at Ramsgate on a Naval Base."

"Good, follow me..."

So I followed him, wondering what the hell I had let myself in for.

He took me up to the 'Holy of Holies' on the ship, the Bridge. The officer approached a Merchant Navy Officer and said, "I think I have found you someone who should be suitable, he's an ex Air Sea Rescue wireless operator."

The Merchant Navy Officer gave me an Aldis Lamp and, pointing to a ship nearby, said, "Call that ship and say 'Dimpy fourth column two."

I looked at him. "D-I-M-P-Y?" I asked.

"Good Lad. Correct spelling is 'D-J-Y-M-P-I' – it's a Polish ship."

I called the ship and the message was accepted.

The Merchant Navy officer turned to the RAF officer and said, "This chap will do fine, he has good speed."

The RAF officer then left.

The Merchant Navy officer then outlined my duties and my watches and hours. He told me the *Stratheden* would be the convoy commander during the voyage and all orders and signals would emanate to and from it.

The following morning the huge convoy put to sea. We went round the North of Ireland and far out into the Atlantic. I thought we must be heading for America, but then the convoy turned South on what was known as a 'zig-zag course'.

---

[1] *Editor's note*: The ferry port town of Gourock sits on the south bank of the Firth of Clyde, 28 miles west of Glasgow.

At regular intervals, on a signal from the *Stratheden*, the whole convoy would change course. This course change signal was sent by a series of flags, hooked on a line and then run up for the rest of the convoy to see. Although I was never trained on flags in the RAF, I became quite adept at running these flags up and reading the signal flags on the other ships, but my main form of signalling was with the ten-inch Aldis Lamp.

The plus side to my signalling duties meant that I was excused 'bullshit atigues' which consisted of scrubbing and polishing anything and everything to keep the men occupied.

The Atlantic can be very rough, especially in winter. Most of the troops were not used to rough seas and suffered from 'mal-de-mer' but this didn't bother me after my service on the Air Sea Rescue launches. There were twelve men on our mess table and for nearly a week I could have had twelve meals at every sitting because I was the only one who eagerly looked forward to mealtimes.

We eventually made a mostly southerly course and when we eventually sailed into warmer climes lots of the lads tried to 'get their knees brown' and spent a lot of time sunbathing. This meant a lot were reporting sick through sunburn (in those days people usually did not travel abroad and therefore had no idea how strong the sun can be in equatorial regions). After nearly a week of this, an order was posted that anyone reporting sick through sunburn would henceforth be put on a charge for 'self-inflicted injury'.

Our 'tropical wear' must have been relics of the Indian Mutiny. We looked like a bunch of comic opera soldiers, but it was all we had and we had to wear it. As the weather became hotter, especially at night, it became fairly uncomfortable below deck, so I would take my blanket up to the gun turret on the bridge and sleep there.

Our first port of call was Freetown, West Africa, but no one was allowed ashore except for the necessary officers to arrange replenishments for the convoy. So for about a week we sweated it out there whilst little boats chugged back and forth with an assortment of supplies. Then onwards we sailed, with no incidents apart from a submarine scare, but thank goodness nothing more.

There were plenty of activities arranged for the troops (apart from the bullshit fatigues) and one of these was an inter-services boxing competition. I had become friendly with two Wireless Operators who had been to Yatesbury together and one told me that his mate had won the boxing championship at Yatesbury and had put his name down for the competition but couldn't get a sparring partner. I said that I was just an ex-lads club boxer but was quite willing to give him a warm up. So we got the gloves on and I told his mate to time us on three one-minute rounds. It took me about fifteen seconds to get the measure of my opponent. He was tall, strong, but a bit on the slow side and in another fifteen seconds I had him where I could hit him at will.

He dropped his hands after a short session of this and said 'stop' and took his gloves off. He took his gloves to hand them back in and then went and crossed his name off the list. I asked him why had done that and he said, "If I meet someone like you at my own weight, I'll get murdered. Why don't you go in for it?"

"I've got more sense mate!" I said.

When I was in Ramsgate I sparred with a lad who had entered the Southern Command boxing competition and unintentionally I caught him with a blow that stopped him in his tracks. I started to apologize but he said, "Look, never apologize when you are boxing, box on..."

After that, he 'stepped up a gear' and gave me one hell of a boxing lesson. When we had finished and were recovering I asked him, "Whose stable were you in before the war?"

"Freddie Mills. I was one of his sparring partners."

"Blimey," I said. "No wonder you gave me a good hiding!"

After that, I decided to lead as quiet a life as possible whilst in the RAF.

We continued our journey round past Cape Town and on to Durban. As we neared Durban, the HMS *Devonshire*, a naval destroyer accompanying our convoy, called us up. She must have been at least twenty miles away and her ten-inch lamp looked like the light from a small torch.

The message was extremely long and gave details of the order of entry into harbour and ended by the captain of the *Devonshire* inviting the captains in the convoy to a meeting and dinner onboard his ship when docked in Durban. In reply our captain sent a long message to the bridge to be sent to the *Devonshire*.

I started to send at a good speed but the signaller on the *Devonshire* must have been one of the best. I speeded up so that in the end I could barely read it myself and yet he still received it perfectly. I would like to have met that signaller!

We entered Durban two days later and remained there for about a month. A lot of troops disembarked and went to a transit camp, apparently for transport on to North Africa. I still had some signalling duties, but not as demanding as while we were at sea, and I got a lot of free time to explore Durban.

The people were exceptionally friendly and I discovered the famous 'Lady in White'[1] who sang all the convoys in and out. She stood on the harbour wall with a megaphone and her singing was so powerful she could command the attention of a whole convoy of troops and received a tremendous applause that must have been heard all over Durban.

❖ ❖ ❖

[1] See Appendix 7 Durban's Lady in White.

~ Chapter 6 ~

INDIA ~ 1943-45

Eventually, on we sailed, and once at sea we were informed that our destination was Bombay. This leg of the voyage was uneventful but hot and sticky. Once we had disembarked at Bombay a truck took us to a transit camp to await our posting.

One of the first wireless operators to be posted thought someone was having a joke with him. The name of the place was somewhere nobody had heard of and he got a rail warrant, and a 'chitty' (pass) for an elephant. I never found out what happened to him.

The following morning, we were on parade and an Army Officer and an RAF Officer came to 'sort us out'.

Six Wireless Operators, including myself, were posted to a place called Poona. Two of my fellow postees were my shipboard friends aboard the *Stratheden*. We were taken to Poona by a pickup truck and arrived at an Army camp. We were tented, given a meal and told to be on parade the following morning.

When we assembled for parade, to our surprise we found out that we (the six new arrivals) were the only RAF blokes in the Army camp, and no sign of a wireless set.

The RSM came on parade and gave us a short talk on do's and dont's then he said,

"I don't know what you lot are doing here, or what I am going to do with six RAF Wireless Operators. Hands up those who can't drive."

Remembering my mistake during our retreat in France, I put my hand up. The RSM looked at me and pointing his swagger stick at me said, "Right, you, get in that lorry and drive it."

"but I can't drive sir, I've got my hand up."

"Who do you think you're kidding? Don't tell me your bloody lies. I remember you when you lived up Affetside. I used to drive the Affetside bus and I know your Jim and your mother. Now, get in that truck and drive, and I'll be watching you!"

So I gave up and drove the lorry.

The following day an RAF Signals officer came looking for six wireless operators who seemed to have gone astray. Thankfully he found us and we said goodbye to the Army camp.

The fact that a war was raging all over the world was not as important as the pomp and circumstance needed to impress the importance of the British Raj. From the highest rank to the ordinary serviceman there were native servants, known as bearers. Your assigned bearer would do everything, bring the morning cuppa, clean kit and would even shave you before you got up, if required.

Well, this signals officer took us to a godforsaken place out in the blue. There was a signals cabin and a short walk away was our billet hut. We arranged wireless watches and had the usual bearers 'to do' for us, but it was so boring.

All this way to be bored to death taking Met reports! But looking through the call sign book I noticed a call beginning MHB, so I knew there must be an Air Sea Rescue Boat somewhere. I immediately wrote out an application for posting to Air Sea Rescue and gave it to the officer and he said he would see to it, but in the meantime I was to report to the SWO at the Parsee College, Poona.

So I was sent to a school where some Indian Army officers were having radio instruction and I was sent to help out. I lasted about four hours. Most of the cadets were Sikhs.

The monsoon had just broken and they were all dancing about on the flat roof, naked, enjoying the rain. A bit later I had occasion to go through their dormitory and I couldn't believe my eyes; they were all in bed with one another.

I tipped one or two out and went to the SWO to tell him about them and when I had told what I had done he got very upset. He said that I had better get out quick before there was a riot. He said that it was part of their religion. I was bundled off quickly in a lorry back to the army and tents.

At least the RSM was pleased to see me because he had received a signal from an RAF signals officer who wanted to know where his six wireless operators had got to. He had a signals station to open and no operators. So we thankfully left the Army camp again and off we went in a lorry,

The day after we had put in our applications a signal came through asking for operators rank of LAC (leading Aircraftman) or above, to volunteer for Wingate's second expedition.[1] As all six of us volunteered, they all came through but my application for Air Sea Rescue took priority.

Back to Air Sea Rescue

ONCE AGAIN, I was on the move, this time right across India to South East Asia Command (SEAC), where I was to be for the rest of the war. My posting was to 226 ASRU Chittagong.

I received a rail warrant and had to get a train to Calcutta and then another to Chittagong. The journey to Calcutta took over 36 hours, eventually arriving at Howrah Station.[2] This was an amazing place (and probably still is) which must be one of the world's largest railway stations and contained an equally large number of people.

Eventually I found the services Rail Travel Officer, who told me there were no trains to Chittagong until midday the next day. He told me to go to St James Transit camp. He then looked at my gear, which consisted of a large tin trunk, a large kitbag and various other small bags and said,

[1] See Appendix 6. Wingate's Second Expedition.

[2] *Editor's note*: Howrah, more popularly known as Howrah Station, is one of the busiest train stations in the world. It is located in the city of Howrah, West Bengal, India. About 600 passenger trains pass through the station each day, requiring its 23 platforms and serving more than one million passengers per day.

"It's a hell of a long way to carry all that. Come on, I will get you a rickshaw."

Going to the door, he summoned one of the rickshaw coolies. We piled all my gear onto this flimsy rickshaw and gingerly I climbed onto a frail looking seat. The Rail Travel Officer explained to the Rickshaw driver where I wanted to go and said to me,

"He'll get you there, but don't let the robbing bastard charge you more than five rupees."

Off we went, I sitting awkwardly on this contraption and the poor skinny bloke between the shafts, running as fast as he could. With all the weight and the structure of the apparatus I expected him to be airborne along with the shafts at any moment.

It was quite a long journey to the transit camp but I found it very interesting seeing most of Calcutta on the way. Eventually we arrived at St James's and a bloke at the reception desk took me to a large dormitory and got two bearers to carry all my gear and then he showed me where to eat and where to shower.

After a shower and quite a nice meal I asked him if there was any place to go for a drink. I assumed that pubs would be non-existent in this part of the world. He said the only safe, decent place was called 'The Green Shutters'. All the servicemen made for that bar and one could get a drink of sorts there.

He went out of the door, called a rickshaw and told the driver where I wanted to go, then said to me, "Don't give the robbing bastard any more than two rupees." I was beginning to wonder about the integrity of rickshaw drivers and the policy of not overpaying them!

Apparently, some years after the war, the rickshaw pullers rebelled and practically brought Calcutta to a standstill for better rates.

Inside 'The Green Shutters' were lots of servicemen, some Anglo-Indian girls and quite a few WAACs, but most important was a bar where you could buy a bottle of something that looked like beer and tasted like beer, although I had my doubts.

I took my beer, sat at a table and listened to the 'band' trying to play dance music, which was awful. I was not impressed. I watched the so-called dancers, who were even worse. A medical orderly approached and I cheered up immediately. He was one of the medics from HSL 120 in Ramsgate. We were both very pleased to see each other.

After the pleasantries he asked, "So what are you doing in Calcutta?"

"I am trying to get to Chittagong to join 226 Air Sea Rescue Unit," I replied.

At this he started to laugh. "Don't bother! I am on 226 and the whole crew is in Calcutta to pick up four launches. The unit will be here for about a month because the launches aren't ready. Where are you staying?"

"St James's transit camp."

"Good, so are we. We have our own section and there is a spare bed next to mine, we will get your kit moved and you can join us. We have our own transport and tomorrow I will introduce you to the CO. Let's have another!"

We enjoyed the rest of the evening catching up.

My New Unit – ASR 226

So I joined 226 Air Sea Rescue Unit sooner, and easier, than I expected and I got to my launch the following morning. The launches were American built, known as Miami Class. They were high powered, well equipped, roomy and comfortable and later proved to be very serviceable and good sea boats.

They had powerful Napier Marine engines and could reach speeds of 40-plus knots. The wireless room was very modern with Canadian Marconi radio sets. Although these were powerful, we had some severe teething troubles.

The base where the boats were being fitted was some twenty miles below Calcutta, nearer to the sea, but the open sea was still some 100 miles away. I am not entirely sure of the distance, but I know it took an awful long time to reach the open sea.

Eventually we got to the Bay of Bengal and out into the open sea, where we could begin the sea trials. The signal started out clear with a good strength but after about four hours I began to receive signals back from Control stating that my signals were unreadable.

We returned to the docks and I thoroughly checked the radio set, aerial and anything I could think of to check but could not find anything wrong.

The following day exactly the same sequence of events, the signal was clear to start and then deteriorated after 3-4 hours. On the third day, when the same thing happened I began to understand the problem after noticing the dials on the set.

With the continual charging of batteries, when running, the grid volts were getting too high, what was required was a resistance to cut out the overload.

I designed what may be termed a Heath Robinson solution. I put a variable resistance in the grid volts circuit, this consisted of a length of resistance wire to the value of one Ohm, a piece of smooth wood as a former, I broke the Low Tension circuit and soldered the feeder to one end of the resistor, I soldered a crocodile clip to the set end of the Low Tension circuit.

As soon as the grid volts began to rise over ten on the dial, I brought my resistor into action by clipping the crocodile clip from the set onto the resistor, the grid volts then stabilized. It worked and I was able to continue transmitting clear messages for over 10 hours.

We continued with sea trials for a week and then were declared operational. We returned to our base near Calcutta to complete arrangements to move to Chittagong, which would take about a week to complete. Although we were operational none of the other boats were, they still had communication problems.

One morning during this final week in Calcutta my junior wireless operator (Ginger Pearce, a good friend of mine) came and woke me up saying,"Wake up, there's an officer on deck who wants to talk to you."

When I made it up on deck the officer said, "I want you to call base and ask for signal strength."

I did, and the reply came back 'loud and clear'.

I realized I was talking to a signals officer because he could quite easily read the Morse code message. He then asked me why I could continue with signals when all the other boats had to stop due to poor signal quality. I explained the problem and showed him my makeshift resistance circuit. He seemed very interested, thanked me and said he would return shortly.

A couple of hours later he returned with three other blokes and one started to take photographs of the transmitter, receiver and the rest of the cabin. The blokes then went and the signals officer then turned to me and said, "I was wondering if you would like to join my team. I am in charge of a signals specialist team and I think you could prove very useful to me. I will be setting up in Chunking shortly and I would like you to join me."

"Yes Sir, I would Sir, but I doubt my CO will release me."

"Don't worry Sparks, I will talk to him and let you know."

I still had my doubts, because wireless operators were a fairly rare breed at the time in the Far East, otherwise I would still be in Ramsgate.

Two days later a dispatch rider brought a sealed envelope addressed to me. It was from the signals officer, a letter saying that they were inserting the modification in the grid volts circuit in the form of a rheostat and this would be installed on the other boats with the same problem.

He said that my CO had strongly opposed me joining his team in Chunking, so he (the signals officer) wished me all the best and enclosed one of the photographs of the wireless cabin, showing the transmitter and part of the desk with a picture of

Joan and Colin (my infant son) on it. I was disappointed, but not surprised, and wondered later what might have been!

On to Burma

TWO DAYS LATER we sailed for Chittagong, our operational base. It was a long journey down the Arakan Coast and it gave the crew a good chance to get to know each other and work together as a crew.

Eventually land came into sight and, as we drew nearer, we could see the hills, dark green with the foliage of the trees. The skipper stood on the small bridge and said, "There you are boys, that's Burma."

To tell the truth, I don't think any of us were very impressed.

Eventually, we sailed up a river and arrived at Chittagong, one of the most forlorn looking places I had ever seen. Operating along this coast was very different than the English Channel. Apart from the climate, sharks, mosquitos, etc., the main difference was that the distances were so vast and the area we had to cover became greater as the offensive along the Arakan[1] gained momentum.

The base at Chittagong was a poor choice from the start, and in time it proved fairly useless. There were no proper facilities for supplies and servicing. Due to the vast distances, it was then deemed a good idea to base the rescue boats on 'strategic' islands. This was obviously a sensible idea but after a while we got fed up of catching fish and drinking the juice from small unripe coconuts called 'dahbs'.

It was not unusual to travel for hours to get to a Rendezvous Point and often a "trip" of two or three days was common, so it was necessary for each boat to have two Wireless Operators in order to keep continuous wireless watch, which was essential.

---

[1] *Editor's note*: The Arakan Campaign of 1942–43 was the first tentative Allied attack into Burma, following the Japanese conquest of Burma earlier in 1942, during the Second World War.

A regular message we received was 'beware shoals, your island is uncharted'. Remote islands seemed to play a large part of our lives along the Arakan. It became known as 'island hopping'.

Eventually we found that most of the time we were nearer Calcutta than Chittagong, so after about 12 months we left Chittagong to the large American contingent based there (and they were welcome to it) and we operated from the base near Calcutta, which was where we did the original sea trials.

My final memory of Chittagong was the native drums beating most of the night and the following morning what seemed like the entire native population crossed the river shouting, "Nippon Come! Nippon Come!"

And come they did, in the form of a light Japanese air raid that would hardly have been noticed in England. It seemed to me that parts of India never saw the war. I remember a similar light air raid on Calcutta and from the following press reports one would have thought the city had been razed to the ground.

We did, however, manage to get a 'farewell' present from the Yanks. The Yanks had started to use a warehouse near where our boats were tied up. They would offload their stores and supplies from the supply ships into this warehouse. On the other side of the warehouse was a railway line where the supplies were loaded into rail trucks for onward distribution.

Ginger Pearce and a fitter from Glasgow, Jimmy Wright, were watching this operation with interest. A line of coolies wearing turbans would queue up by the warehouse and an American GI would place a box on their head and then they would walk to the train and another GI would offload the box and put it in the railway truck.

The coolie would then re-join the queue for the next box. Overseeing all this was just one armed GI, and it took him about twenty minutes to complete his circuit round the railway sidings and the warehouse, which he did regularly.

Ginger and Jimmy took their shirts off, wrapped some rag round their heads and, as the guard disappeared, they joined the queue waiting for a box. They blended in very well, as by that time we all had a good tan.

Their turn came to receive a box and the 'bored' GI never noticed the 'European coolies'. They started to make their way towards the railway but at the right time they turned quickly and headed for our boat. They both repeated this operation three or four times and then resumed their position on the boat in time for the guard to re-appear.

The 'booty' from the boxes, mostly tinned food, was then hidden everywhere on the boat, wherever a tin could be hidden. As it went dark the wood from the boxes was broken up and taken to the river, where it was washed out to sea, then we all turned in, satisfied with the day's work.

The following morning, very early, the CO and two very large American Service Policemen boarded the boat.

The CO said, "Did you leave the launch anytime last night Sparks?"

"No Sir, not at all," said I.

"Was anyone with you on board?"

"Yes sir, Ginger and Jock."

One of the big Americans intervened, "Hey! how do you know they didn't leave?"

"Because we were playing brag in the radio room, you will see all my winnings if you care to look, they are matches until we get paid!"

"Well that's strange, the guard said he thought he saw two guys heading this way," the Yank continued.

I decided to take a gamble with the Yank. "Look, if the word of a British NCO is not good enough, come and search the boat, but I will expect an apology."

"Well hell, it beats all!" he said, and they turned and walked away.

A very short time after this we received a crash call and were off!

We set off down the river and into the Bay of Bengal. The pilot had managed to give his position before he ditched and it only took us a few hours to reach the position.

We found the dinghy but it was empty. Despite an intensive search for two days at sea and neighbouring islands, most of which were uninhabited, we never found him.

This situation was not unusual in these waters, for every dinghy we found occupied, we would find two or three unoccupied. This part of the Indian Ocean contained a lot of hungry sharks and the Japanese also had regular patrols.

On one occasion we searched a group of islands, again mostly uninhabited, for an airman reported down. One of the islands we searched had a small native population. When we came across an island such as this, the routine was the always the same, we would land cautiously, in case of a Japanese presence.

The island would at first seem to be deserted, even though there were signs of native habitation. Then, as it was established that we were not Japanese, the children of the island would appear, followed by the women and finally the men!

On this occasion, after the natives had shown themselves, a white man appeared with his leg bandaged and using a rough piece of wood as a crutch.

He hobbled towards us a said he had been on the island for three months. He was not the pilot we were looking for, and we never found our original quarry, but this pilot was relieved to get back into civilization and not run the risk of being discovered by the Japanese.

Fame at Last!

One successful pick-up gained our crew some notoriety. The Americans had been bombing Singapore and one of their bombers had come down a long way into Japanese controlled waters.

Control asked our skipper if a pick-up was possible. He worked out the distance, running time at full speed and where we would need to refuel on the return journey, then told Control it was possible if a refuelling launch could meet us at a pre-arranged position.

This was all confirmed and off we went on a 36-hour outward trip at full speed. The skipper's navigation was spot on as usual and we sighted the dinghy with the crew in it, which was made easier by the fact that the bomber was still floating nearby and after we had rescued the crew it took quite a lot of our deck gun's ammunition before it would sink.

The survival rations the crew had retrieved from the aircraft before they abandoned it were amazing, which added to our store which our two 'bearers' had started. The Americans were always better supplied than British Forces.

The Americans told us that, as we approached, they thought we were a Japanese gunboat and were about to 'take the easy way out' when they saw the RAF roundels on the bows and couldn't believe their luck. They never thought they would be rescued so far into Japanese waters.

We had commenced our return journey and after a while I transmitted details of the pick-up to base as per normal procedure and they then replied and asked for our ETA.

I was a little surprised at this, being so far out, so I asked the skipper for an ETA.

He looked at his watch (by now it was 2pm on a Thursday) and said, "Tell 'em 5.30am Saturday."

I logged this and made a note to myself to check our arrival time.

We dropped our passengers off at our friendly American base at Chittagong and they showed their appreciation by giving us loads of 'goodies' (this time with their blessings) and we returned to our base at Calcutta. We arrived at 5.15am on Saturday!

Some months after we received through the 'post' a copy of an American magazine called 'Life'. We were a little bemused when we received this until we saw the headline, in big black type, 'Descendant of Drake Rescues Life reporter'.

Apparently one of the crew we picked up was a 'Life' magazine war correspondent and it was also news to us that our skipper was indeed a descendant of the famous bowler/sailor from Plymouth, for although he was a direct descendant of Francis Drake, his surname was Cook!

All we knew of him was that before the war he was a schoolmaster and an amateur yachtsman. He was a natural seaman, and only once he was foxed, although it was not his fault, and even then he never lost his sense of humour.

Friendly Fire

ONE NIGHT AS we lay close inshore to an island called Ramree, it was about 2am and there was a bit of a commotion on deck.

The skipper shouted down to me, "Can you come on deck Sparks? Somebody is shooting at us from a gunboat."

I went on deck with a night lamp and gave a ship to ship signal, they were still firing, it was a good job they weren't very accurate. I tried the Aldis lamp and flashed 'RAF', but the gunfire was getting a bit more concentrated. I began to wonder how hungry the sharks were.

Ginger came on deck to see what was happening and after a few short moments he grabbed the loud hailer and said in his cockney voice,

"Stop bleeding shooting at us you stupid bastards, we're an RAF Rescue Craft!"

A bit unorthodox but it worked, the shooting stopped!

At daylight we drew alongside our 'antagonists'. It was an Indian gunboat with a white officer. He apologized for the mistake and I said,

"What's wrong with your signaller? Why didn't he recognize my signal?"

"The stupid bastard had the wrong list out. It's a good job they are totally inept otherwise we would have blown you out of the water."

"Well, there is that about it." said our skipper, starting to see the funny side of it.

"To be fair, we had not been told that a rescue craft would be so close to shore," the officer complained.

As a footnote to this, apparently some time later, a large Japanese force of approximately 1,000 men attempted to cross the marshes and river close to the location of this incident, and only approximately 19 survived, the crocodiles had the rest.[1]

While we were tied up in Calcutta, the RN ship HMS *Dorsetshire* came into harbour. As we watched her glide into the harbour near us, I have never felt so proud to have, in a small way, worked with her. On the foredeck, all dressed in spotless whites, was the Marine Band playing. It was a marvellous sight.

Rest and Recuperation?

THE CO RECEIVED a message from HQ to rest a convenient number of units, and as our launch was due for a major overhaul which would take approximately six weeks, the CO decided that myself, Ginger Pearce and the relief wireless operator, Jock Slater, were sent on a 'Hill Party' for 'rest and recuperation'. Two of the crew had already been on one of these trips to Darjeeling and had a great time, so we were looking forward to it.

So off we went, not to Darjeeling but to a place called Shillong. The journey consisted of a 12-hour train journey to the railhead, where we were given a meal and told to get some sleep because we would be leaving early in the morning, and we were directed to a little tent.

We settled down and were woken at 4am, given a quick breakfast and told to board a convoy of lorries. As I was an NCO I was put in charge of one of the lorries, which meant I could

[1] See Appendix 7. The Ramree Massacre.

travel in the cab next to the driver, a situation I didn't appreciate until later in the journey.

We soon started to climb into the hills, up and up we went and the switchback road dwindled into a narrow track which twisted and turned, winding its way upwards. The vegetation changed from tropical to sub-tropical and eventually temperate pine forest. Occasionally the convoy had to pull into passing places to allow convoys coming down the hill to pass. Eventually we arrived at the camp.

The hills we were in were known has the Shan hills and we were told that the Shan tribe, something like the Gurkhas in build, were still head-hunters less than 50 years before.

The first thing that struck me was the large number of Service Police, both British and American, and we soon found out why. When the 'guests' arrived after the tiring 'white knuckle' journey and saw the foreboding rock face rise above the camp, then look back at the drop off the road of hundreds of feet with the wreckage of a lorry that didn't make one of the bends at the bottom, many thought they would be better off walking back to their units!

From where we stood we could look over the hills to the mountains in the far distance, one of which, we were told, was Everest. It looked a nice walk to get there, but we were told that it was over twenty miles away.

We were assigned to a native hut or 'basha', given eight blankets each and told to ask for more if we felt cold, and then we were given a talk by the Medical Officer, who told us to take it easy for a week to get used to the thin air at this altitude. Then an officer gave us the usual talk about 'dos and donts'. The main 'don't' being don't mix with the local girls or enter the native huts.

The local natives belonged to the Khasi tribe, who were reputed to have the most beautiful girls in the world, and there were some Allied losses to these girls in the area. Some servicemen went through the local marriage ceremony then promptly disappeared into the hills and became impossible to find.

After a few days of resting, the activities started. A hunting party was organized but when we saw the way some of them handled the guns Ginger and I decided to go fishing!

We were given fishing rods and told to join the fishing party in a lorry. We were first to be dropped off after a thankfully short journey and directed to a river. We soon found a nice spot and settled down to a restful day's fishing.

Eventually I got a bite. It was quite a large fish and it took me a while to land it. When I did, I had no idea what sort of fish it was, it was large and but as it lay on the bank it actually 'barked' at me.

Some locals who passed by on the river told us it was a type of catfish, but I had never seen or heard anything like that. Anyway, we asked them if they would like it, which they thankfully accepted. As the afternoon drew on, we packed our gear and made our way back to the road.

A local passed by, carrying two large birds that seemed to belong to the pheasant family but were larger than any pheasants I had seen. He also carried a bow and a quiver with about half a dozen arrows in it. I asked him if he had shot the birds with the bow and arrow and he looked at me strangely, probably thinking it was obvious, but then he grinned and said he had. I then asked him what distance he was from the birds. He took two strides and counted out thirty-five on his fingers.

I emptied a cigarette packet and stuck it on a tree. I then counted out 35 strides and asked him if he could hit the cigarette packet. Three arrows hit the packet dead centre as fast as any revolver.

Satisfied with the quality of the bow and arrows, I asked him if he would sell me his bow and arrows and what he wanted for it. He indicated that he wanted five packets of cigarettes. Ginger and I managed to find the cigarettes between us and he left, happily smoking.

He would have probably made another one before the day was out, but we were delighted with our buy and Ginger and I spent many happy hours trying to improve our archery skills at two tin cans. The bow and arrows were made out of cane and the arrows had steel tips and were deadly once we got the hang of it. When we eventually did hit a tin can it went straight through it!

There was an American rest camp next to ours and Ginger and I got to know a couple of Yanks. One day they asked us if we would like to go to a concert on their camp, which we gladly accepted, anything to break the monotony, so Ginger and I went to this concert hall in the American camp.

The place was filling up and the band was busy setting up their equipment on the stage. One of the bandsmen asked if there was an electrician in the audience and one of the Americans who had invited us pointed to me and said, "Yeah, this guy here."

The bandsman asked me if I could figure out why his electric 'vibro-thing' didn't work. I looked at the wiring under this thing and found a wire that seemed to be doing nothing and then found another one that seemed to be doing the same.

I borrowed a knife, scraped the two ends, and joined them together. I told the bandsman to try the instrument and there was no one more pleased than I was when it worked. That small service got us much better seats.

When the band started to play, I kept saying to Ginger, "Hey, this band's not bad."

"Yeah, good beat," replied Ginger.

"Who is this band playing, they're quite good?" I asked one of our hosts.

He seemed a little hurt and surprised and said, "You're kidding me, this is Glen Miller's band."

That was the first time I had heard of Glen Miller and I was saddened to hear of his tragic end some time later, but I felt very proud then, and even more proud as his fame spread, that I had once repaired a bit of his band.

In the basha I slept near to the door and Ginger slept next to Jock. On the second night Ginger woke me up to tell me Jock was walking in his sleep and was making for the open door. As I have explained, the camp was situated on a hillside with a large drop on the other side of the road, so anyone sleepwalking could easily go over the edge.

Also tiger tracks had been seen near the cookhouse and if Jock wandered into the bush at night he probably would have been attacked. I gently led Jock back to his bed. After that we worked out a warning system when Jock started to walk.

One morning I suggested to Jock that he reported sick. He said he felt alright and saw no need to go sick. I told him about his taking a walk in the night, which surprised him. I told him he would be better off if he left Air Sea Rescue because if he took a walk when we were at sea at night, there was a good chance he would not be noticed, and if he walked off the boat there could be a hungry shark or two hanging about.

He said he didn't want to leave Air Sea Rescue and if he stayed with me he would do all the night watches so that if he walked during the day he would be noticed, and that arrangement stood right up to when 226 ASR unit was disbanded.

Our rest and recuperation over, we started our long journey back to base. Well stocked up with bottles of rum to calm our nerves for the journey back down the hills, off we went. The journey was equally long and uneventful as the journey out.

Lost at Sea

BACK ON THE boat, one night we were running back to base overnight, it was about 11.pm when the skipper told the coxswain the course and to wake him about 3.am. The skipper then went to get a bit of sleep and the fitter joined the cox in the wheelhouse and had a chat.

Two of the crew were out on deck as lookouts when one shouted to the cox, 'breakers ahead', then the other lookout shouted, 'breakers to port', then 'beakers to starboard'. There were breakers all round when we should have been in very deep water.

The cox stopped the launch and sent for the skipper. The skipper looked round and said to my Wireless Operator, who was on duty, "Now Ginger, what would you do in a situation like this?"

Ginger, a Cockney with a great sense of humour, said immediately, "Drop the bleeding hook and wait until daylight sir."

It seemed that was the answer the skipper wanted, because that's just what he did.

When daylight came we were amazed to find that we were in the middle of a lagoon with breakers all around us, except for the narrow entrance through which we had fortunately come in.

The skipper and the cox studied the chart and couldn't work out where we were, or how we had got there. Slowly we came out of the lagoon and the skipper said to me,

"Now Sparks, is the time to prove that that box of tricks you have is of some use. Can you direct us to some point we can work from?"

The 'box of tricks' he referred to was the new Radio Direction Finding System which I had previously completed a course on. I switched on the RDF and swung the loop aerial until I picked up a signal from a radio beacon I recognised. I turned to the skipper and said, "Will Patenga do sir?"

"That will be fine, I can find my way from there."

So for the next 12 hours or so I sat with my eyes glued to the small screen giving the order 'port' or 'starboard' to keep homing in on that beacon.

Eventually the skipper came to me, looking relieved, and said, "I don't know much about your box of tricks Sparks, but we know where we are now. Oh, by the way, you are just one degree out. Bloody good show! Switch off and get your head down."

I needed no further telling. I left Ginger on the radio and gratefully rested my eyes. The reason for the navigational error? The fitter talking to the cox had a spanner in his pocket and of course the cox followed the direction of the compass needle, which was slightly deflected.

A Secret Mission

BACK AT BASE we were doing a lot of patrols to cover the landings down the Arakan coast. We had just returned from one patrol and the CO was waiting. He told me to get my small kit, saying that he had received a signal asking for the senior operator to report at once as directed. Transport was waiting to take me to some 'ghat' (landing stage), higher up the river.

The driver dropped me some twenty miles up-river. Moored in a remote spot was a Pinnace, where a Wing Commander met me, took me aboard and declared to an assembled group of officers that I was the 'Sparks'.

Apart from myself and a Sergeant Marine Fitter, the lowest rank among those on board was the Wing Commander. There were Army, Navy and Air Force officers on board and I was puzzled as to what was going on.

The Naval Officer showed me the wireless cabin, a very elaborate affair compared to ASR launches. He then gave me a frequency to set up on and handed me a code book that I had never seen before. Almost immediately, we set sail down river.

The Naval Officer told me get a frequency check and signal strength. Both satisfactory, I was told to keep a listening watch until 7.pm and then close down until 8am. No other orders and no questions. That was the routine for the next two days.

The pinnace was much slower than the ASR launches but very comfortable despite the slight overcrowding. I don't know who did the cooking, but it was very unusual to be served nice food by an officer.

On the third day we had crossed the Bay of Bengal and were going down the Arakan coast. Eventually we came to three large barges moored near the coast and tied up alongside the first one.

The Wing Commander told me to go with him on the first barge. We went below and I was amazed at the elaborate setup and the luxury of it. It was a complete radar station, brimming with modern, probably top secret, equipment including a high-tech radio. The station appeared to be fully manned but the Wing Commander told me to help test the signals equipment.

We didn't go on the other barges but I assumed they would be the living quarters. When we had completed our checks we went back onto the Pinnace and continued our journey. After we had set off, the Wing Commander told me I must never mention what I had seen to anyone, not even my CO.

We continued on down the Arakan Coast for another four days and the Naval Officer gave me a coded message to transmit. Shortly after sending the message, we turned up a very narrow creek, overgrown by the jungle. We had travelled what seemed like quite a long way up the creek and then the engines stopped.

The Army officer told the Sergeant fitter and myself to camouflage the boat thoroughly, which we did, and we were told to use what rations we needed to eat. The Naval Officer gave me the time to listen to the signals and the code signs and with that the officers disappeared into the jungle, leaving just myself and the Sergeant Fitter.

We had a lot of time to ourselves and to relieve the boredom we took turns to swim in the creek next to the boat. On the second day there was a hell of a crashing in the jungle near us, and a DUKW (an amphibious vehicle), crashed through the jungle and into the creek about 50 yards from us.

A large white American was driving it and an even larger black American manning a pair of machine guns on the rear. It crossed the creek and disappeared back into the jungle, we must have been well camouflaged because they never noticed us, or just weren't interested.

The officers came back on the third day and we removed the camouflage and started up the engines to make our way back to the sea. When the engines started up I was at the stern of the pinnace and among the disturbance of the water I saw two big black water snakes come up to the surface, in the same spot we had been swimming!

When we got back to the ghat we had started from, I gathered my small kit to get on the same vehicle that had brought me. Before I left, the Wing Commander reminded me that if ANYONE, including my CO, asked where I'd been or what we did, I was just to say that we had been on a trip but not sure where, which is just what I told my CO.

Using Sound Advice

I HAD OCCASION to recall the words of wisdom the Naval Signals Officer in Ramsgate told me about the responsibility for signals at sea being solely that of the Wireless Operator.

It was the first trip out with a new skipper, whose navigation and management skills were, to say the least, suspect. I remarked quietly that I didn't think he could navigate the Bolton-Bury canal.

After a fruitless search in response to a crash call, when we weren't even sure if we were searching the correct area, he decided it was time to call off the search and return to base. We had been searching close inshore and had been there quite a time when an aircraft flew over, not showing any lights and it could not be positively identified.

Jock was on wireless watch and the skipper told Jock, "Send unidentified aircraft passed overhead."

I said to Jock, "Do no such thing."

The skipper, taken aback said, "What has this got to do with you? You're not on watch."

I turned to Jock and said to the skipper, "I've just taken over watch, Jock, make an entry in the log book."

"Now sir," I said, turning to the skipper, "You was saying something about breaking radio silence to report an unidentified aircraft. I am sorry I cannot carry out that order for two reasons. First, wherever that aircraft is going, it will probably be there by now, and second, radar stations will have picked up that aircraft a long ago."

The skipper said, "You know you are in trouble for refusing to obey the orders of an officer, and how do you know about the radar stations? I've never heard of any down this coast."

"I just know about the radar stations. How I know is of no concern, you will have to ask the CO." I logged everything down along with the times. We then set off back to base.

For the skipper this was easier said than done. We seemed to cover the entire Bay of Bengal and he still couldn't get his bearings. To make things worse the sea started to add to his problems by cutting up rough.

The skipper asked me to get him a fix, which I did. He didn't seem happy with this and asked for another, which I did, and continued this every few minutes for about half an hour. Then he announced the fixes were wrong, although these were cross fixes, which could usually be relied on as accurate.

"Sparks, that last fix you gave me puts s on top of a mountain!"

"Maybe there is a mountain underneath us in the water," I said helpfully.

"Base wants to know if we are in trouble, should I tell them we are on top of a mountain, Sir?"

Just at that time the a fitter came in and asked the skipper, "Can you tell me how long before we reach Base Sir?"

"You had better ask Sparks, he's the one getting the fixes, I am not sure."

The fitter replied, "Well somebody had better find out because we are bloody low on fuel."

By now the sea was getting really rough. I took one look at the damn big waves and put on my Mae West, the first and only time I used it. The skipper disappeared below and the Cox (an ex Grimsby trawlerman) stepped in.

"Get me just one fix Sparks," he said.

I got the fix and handed it to him. He looked at the chart on the chart table, threw it on the floor and said, "He had the wrong bloody chart open!"

He got another chart out, did some calculations, went to the wheel and seemed to turn the launch round on top of a big wave and we soon arrived back at Base with just enough fuel, a masterpiece of seamanship.

When we got within sight of the base, which now was the one below Calcutta, the skipper took my log book and told me I was on a charge. When we eventually docked there was a reception committee. As normal procedure I had sent an ETA as soon as the Cox had sorted out our problem and was able to give me a time.

There was a Group Captain, a Wing Commander and our CO. The CO asked for my log book and told the skipper and the Cox to join him and the other officers and off they went in a jeep.

A couple of hours later the skipper, the CO and the signals officer came back to the launch and called me ashore.

The CO said, "Sparks, here is your log book and this officer (the skipper) owes you an apology."

I felt a bit embarrassed at that and said to the CO, "with all due respect Sir, no apology is called for, the Skipper did his duty has he saw it and I did mine as I knew it should be done."

The Signals officer said, "Now tell me why you were so sure of yourself in refusing to transmit a signal ordered by an officer, and how, and what do you know about the radar stations?"

I replied, "To answer the first question, I had occasion in the English Channel to contradict an order from a senior officer and the Naval Officer in charge of signals told me in no uncertain terms what my responsibilities were. For the second question you will have to ask my Commanding Officer, I am not allowed to do so, on orders from a higher authority."

The CO smiled and said, "Thank you Sparks, that is all, carry on with whatever you were doing."

We never saw that skipper again.

Not long after this incident there was a big push down the Arakan, both inland and down the coast but, unfortunately, I went into hospital for the third and last time with malaria.

We had run out of Mepacrine, the tablets which held malaria in check, and I had been able to hold it off with a bottle of whisky, but when I had used all that up I was hit pretty hard. I don't remember much about the journey to hospital in Calcutta but I know it took longer than before to get over it and get well enough to go back to operations.

On one of the last trips I did we had been sitting on a Rendezvous Point for a while and it was quite a way down the coast, things were quiet, little or no signals and we were debating whether to go for a swim.

We put the crash nets out and two volunteers were selected to stand on deck with rifles to keep nosey sharks away and just as we were about to dive in the skipper bobbed his head out of the water and said, "What are you all waiting for?" He had quietly slipped over the other side of the boat and swam under it. That decided us and we all dived in.

Back to Calcutta

SHORTLY AFTERWARDS IT was time for another refit and the boat was put on stocks. All the Wireless Operators were sent to an RAF station called Ranchi, where they were having difficulties with their signals and we were told to go and sort it out. The base was a bomber base, run mostly by the Indian Air Force.

The camp's entire communications was a mess, we soon fixed the telephone to the control tower. We then tuned the radio sets to the correct frequency for the bombing range and established proper communications procedures.

The ground crew told me they were pretty fed up with having to repair aircraft which had not been damaged in combat. The Indian pilots flying the squadron of Blenheim bombers were very inexperienced and for every aircraft successfully touched down on the landing strip, two ended up on the grass, usually with damage to the undercarriage.

On the third day an American Mitchell Bomber landed and the Flying Control Officer asked if I could tune his radio to the correct frequency. When I climbed into the cockpit, I got the shock of my life. Pointing through the nose of the aircraft a large cannon had been rigged up, which was belt fed and the belt was arranged to wind its way round the aircraft in what appeared to be a clever arrangement, although I don't think I would have trusted it to work in a dogfight!

Having recovered my composure, I looked at the radio set, which reminded me of the course I completed at Cranwell, it was crystal controlled and as I had completed a course on it I was soon able to tune it to the correct frequency. It was even easier because this model was push button controlled. I called the control Tower and told the Flying Control officer all was in order. He seemed very pleased with my efficient work, so I decided to be a bit cheeky.

On the tarmac was a transport plane which I knew was soon taking off for Calcutta, so I asked the Flying Control Officer if there was any chance of a lift. He agreed, but said I would have to hurry as it was about to leave in ten minutes.

I broke the sprint record to the billet, got my gear and just managed to scramble aboard before it set off. I told the other Wireless Operators that I was going to see the CO to get us all returned to our unit and away from this 'suicide squad'.

I had no trouble getting from Calcutta airport to our base and reported immediately to the CO. Somehow, he didn't seem surprised to see me.

"Well Sparks, what's the problem?" he enquired.

"The problem, Sir, is those Indian pilots. If you don't recall us all, you will have a set of Wireless Operators with a nervous disability."

"OK Sparks, leave it with me," he said. He obviously took on board what I had told him because the next day the remaining Wireless Operators gratefully returned to base.

End of the War in Southeast Asia – August 1945

THINGS WERE FAIRLY quiet for a while, then one day we were tied up next to an American Corvette. There was a lot of talk and excitement when it was rumoured that the Americans had dropped an Atom bomb on the Japanese, then it was rumoured that they had dropped a second one, and we knew that the end of the war must be very close.

On the day that the declaration of the Japanese surrender was expected an officer from the Corvette asked if I could help out. Their loudspeaker system had gone wrong and their Sparks had gone sick that morning. It was a simple loose wire and after about ten minutes I had sorted out the problem, so all onboard could hear the important announcement of VJ Day.

The Captain of the US naval vessel asked who had fixed the broadcast system and when told that it was the Sparks from the RAF rescue boat alongside he gave the order for 'neaters' to be given and that I was to be included. One of the crew gave me a mug and the bosun, who was dishing out the rum, gave me a generous measure and then another sailor came along and filled my mug up once more with rum.

When I had drunk all this, I was walking on cloud nine. Then it was mess time and a massive meal was put in front of me. By the time I had eaten it, and drunk another mug of rum, all I wanted to do was to have a kip, so I stretched out on a bunk and slept for quite a time. When I awoke I thanked the naval lads for their hospitality, and went back on my own boat.

The cox told me that the skipper had been on board and had asked where I was. When told that I was last seen going aboard the American Naval vessel to do a repair job, the skipper seemed happy with this and left.

After over four years in the Far East we were all grateful that the war against the Japanese had been brought to a swift end, albeit by a terrible weapon. We were also grateful to the atom bombs for saving thousands of Allied lives in not having to fight a fanatical enemy all the way to Tokyo. We were now all wondering how long it would be before we could think about returning home.

A few days later we heard that 226 was to be disbanded and I handed back all the equipment I had signed for. A dinner was proposed and the cook said that if we gave him some money to buy the food he would put on a dinner on we wouldn't forget.

For a long time the only food he had available to feed us with was terrible, so we naturally were a little sceptical as to his ability to put on a really good dinner, but we decided to give him a chance and raised some money for some decent ingredients.

He went on to prove he was indeed able to cook good food when allowed, and he put on a dinner which was out of this world, especially after all that time on RAF supplied rations. Some meals were so awful when we returned from a trip we couldn't eat them but when we challenged the quality of food he supplied he said that with the rations he was given he couldn't do any different.

After the dinner I asked him what he did in civvy street and he told me he was a chef at a top London hotel, the name of which I have forgotten.

The night was a huge success. The cook gave us all a menu, nicely laid out (tongue in cheek) and nicely printed. Each of us signed each other's menu.

Talk now was of when we would get our release number and start making our long way home. My release group was one of the first to come through and I was duly ordered to report to HQ Calcutta to be cleared from India.

For the last two years I had adopted a stray dog, which I had become quite attached to and he used to welcome me when I returned to base and while I was away from base the other lads between them looked after him.

A local Anglo-Indian family I had become acquainted with said they would be happy to adopt him, so I was relieved that he was going to a good home. That sorted, I packed the rest of my belongings in my tin trunk and the Chippy painted on it, "NOT WANTED ON VOYAGE".

The following morning I reported to HQ, dressed smarter than at any time since I had been out there, because I knew I had to see the Group Captain for my last bit of paperwork. But before I even got into the building a Warrant Officer (Discipline) pulled me up.

"Sergeant, why are you improperly dressed?"

I was taken aback, as I had taken a lot of trouble to dress correctly.

"Sorry Sir, what is improper about my dress?"

"You are not showing your campaign ribbons."

"I do not have any campaign ribbons," I replied.

"I suggest you check the Notice Board, read the POR's (Personal Occurrence Reports) then go to the stores, draw the ribbons, then go to the Durhzi Walla (tailor) and get them sewn on."

When I had done this I was very surprised at what I had qualified for. I received the 1939/45 Star, Atlantic Star, Burma Star and the Defence medal. Later I received two more medals. When I got to Bombay I obtained another set of the above ribbons to put on my blues.

I was documented, paid and interviewed by the Group Captain, who gave me my Release Book. All I had to do after that was to get a train to Bombay and await embarkation on 'THAT BOAT'.

The train was full of Servicemen, naturally "demob happy". By the time the train reached Bombay it was a wonder there was any train left, but arrive we did, and we were taken to that same Transit Camp where we started our "Far East Journey". But this time we weren't waiting to be posted, full of apprehension at what lay ahead, we could look forward to going home to our families.

In the camp were a lot of newcomers, waiting for their postings. We looked on them with pity, but at least the hostilities were over. Every morning we paraded at 9 o'clock and for a month the Sergeant would come out and say, "Not today lads, see you nine in the morning," and off we would go to while away another day.

The main place where we spent our time was a sort of European Club at a place called Beach Candy, (or Beach Kandy), I never was sure which. There we could swim, eat, drink and generally laze about. Years later I saw this club featured on television as an item in 'Whicker's World'.

On My Way Home

EVENTUALLY THE LONG-AWAITED day came. We were told to put our gear and ourselves in the waiting lorries, our boat had arrived, the RMS *Mooltan*. [see Appendix 8]

As the ship set off, we all crowded on deck to see the Gateway of India disappear in the distance, some staying until it was no longer visible to make sure it was really gone, many of us hoping never to return.

What a difference the return trip was. It was like a holiday cruise (not that many of us had enjoyed such a luxury at that time), there were no fatigues, parades or duties, we could just relax.

This time we went through the Suez Canal, I suppose it was too dangerous on the way out. As we were coming through the Suez Canal we ran aground. As we were all standing on deck watching the fruitless efforts of small boats to get us free, I joked with one of the lads that when we ran aground with the rescue launch we rocked it clear.

One day I was walking round the deck and who should I encounter but an officer who was once my skipper. He was talking to a Wing Commander and my old skipper introduced me to him.

The Wing Commander asked me where I had served on Air Sea Rescue apart from the Far East, and when I told him I was stationed in Ramsgate he asked me if I met some girl and mentioned her name. I did not recall the name, but when he mentioned her parents had a farm near Manston airfield I recognized the girl as the one I knew as 'The Killer'. I said I had once met a girl who was the daughter of a farmer at Manston and he asked me to describe the girl.

This, of course, was not difficult and I gave a vivid description of her blonde hair, how she was very vivacious and a figure that would put any film star in the shade. He said "Yes that's the girl, that is..." and said the girl's name again (which I still cannot recall).

"Oh yes," I replied enthusiastically, "I never knew her name, we always called her the Manston Killer."

The Wing Commander then replied, a little haughtily, "She is my fiancée!"

There was a short, embarrassing silence, which was broken by my old skipper's laughter and he chortled, "Sparks I think you've dropped a clanger!"

Fortunately, I never saw either of them again. I often wondered if the Wingco did marry the Killer.

I had hardly finished speaking when over the Tannoy came a voice ordering everyone on deck and assemble on one side of the ship. Then came the order, 'When I say jump, altogether, Jump, and Jump...'

This continued for a few minutes and everybody was laughing and jumping like mad, and then came the voice, 'Thank you gentlemen, we are now clear of the sandbank.'

Everybody gave a big cheer and slowly dispersed, still laughing and joking about the situation.

It is hard to describe the euphoria and the general feeling among the troop passengers of that ship, life was good and we were going home in a peaceful world. When we passed another ship after dark it was a great sight to see it with all its lights on.

When we were passing the Bitter Lakes we saw a building and on the wall, in big letters, was the message, 'The home of the Desert Rats 8th Army'.

There was a big cheer as everybody saw it, and then by the side of the lake in swimsuits we saw white girls, the first many of us had seen for four years. They were with what we presumed were part of the Desert Rats.

At this the cheers changed to whistles for the girls and ribald comments for the men, such as 'no wonder you don't want to go home', and 'get some in'.

Before we had completely passed them we gave them a final cheer. Some of the final comments were, 'White girls, you lucky buggers!'

On a more sombre side, in solemnity, we held a very moving service in memory of those lads we had left back there in the jungle.

Coming through the 'Med' we found the weather somewhat cooler after having acclimatized to tropical conditions and we changed from tropical dress to our 'ordinary' uniform, and the wake of the ship was littered with well-worn bush shirts, shorts, and hats.

Very soon the ship was coming up the river Mersey. It was the end of November 1945.

On our mess deck I had got friendly with two lads, one came from Stoke and the other from Tonge Moor, Bolton. I told them that when we saw the Liver Buildings I would open a bottle of whisky I had carried all the way from Calcutta.

One of the finest sights and memories I have ever had was seeing the Liver Building domes, covered with snow, come into view and the three of us emptying that bottle of whisky.

When we disembarked at Liverpool there was a band playing, WVS ladies dashing around with tea, sandwiches, cakes, and cigarettes, and assisted by, of all people, Military and Service Police.

We were taken to Lime Street station and helped onto a train and as the train pulled out of the station people cheered and we were on our way to – of all places – RAF Blackpool!

There we had another reception committee and were taken to civilian billets. We were told it would only be for a day or so before the demob centre was ready to process us.

The lad from Tonge Moor was in the same bedroom as me and he watched me putting some bits and pieces in my side bag.

"What are you doing?" he asked.

"I haven't travelled 7,000 miles and been away over four years to be stuck 30 miles from home."

"How are you going to get back for the 8 a.m. parade?"

"Easy, 6am workman's train Bolton to Preston and bus from Preston gets us back in Blackpool in time for parade."

So he decided to come with me. At Blackpool station we were told we had a wait of two hours for a train to Bolton, so we went in a nearby pub. A Yank came to the bar and stood next to us.

We got talking and I told him I had met a lot of American servicemen and that we were grateful to them. I didn't elaborate about the pilfered supplies, half a truth was good enough. The Yank seemed pleased and he was very generous in buying drinks, right up to the time for our train.

We arrived at the barrier and two SPs spotted us and started towards us. I was rapidly thinking up a good reason hy we were going for a train, but the two SP's said, "We have had strict orders not to bother you lads just back from the Far East.'

So we got the train to Bolton. We decided to share a taxi, seeing I was making for Bradshaw and he lived on Tonge Moor, which was on the way. The last letter I had received from Joan gave the address Bradshaw Hall Farm Cottage, so I asked the taxi drive to take me to that address.

The house was in darkness and there was no answer to my knocking, so I decided to try the pub. Neither Joan nor my mother had been there, so I decided to try our Jim's up Affetside.

I told them what had happened and Cathy, my cousin, said she would go with me. Apparently while I had been making my way home from India, the family had moved house.

So finally I had found my family. I asked the taxi driver to take Cathy home and asked him how much I owed him. He said that that ride was on him, seeing I had just come home from the Far East.

Have you ever seen those films on the telly, the old black and white ones, where the wandering warrior returns to his family and everybody falls on the hero's neck and smothers him with kisses? Well don't you believe it! After four years away, one hell of a job to find where I lived, and when I entered the house, the following rapport occurred...

Mother: "Look who's here."

Wife: "Oh, its you."

Well, it was nice to be home, if only for a few hours!

Demob

THE FOLLOWING MORNING we caught the train and bus and got back to Blackpool in good time. After parade we were put on a train to Hednesford to be demobbed. On arrival we were given blankets and directed to some huts.

It was the middle of winter, there was no heating in the huts, and we had just returned from a tropical climate, so we all spent a miserable cold night, but still, the next day we would be civilians.

The following morning, a Saturday, a Sergeant appeared and told us that we wouldn't be processed until Monday, as the WAAF who did some of the paperwork was on weekend leave.

I will always remember what 300 war-weary angry airmen look like!

We marched into the COs office and told the SWO to bring him out. Eventually he came out and various spokesmen from our group asked him why, just because one WAAF had got the weekend off, we had to starve to death and freeze in bloody cold huts, until Monday.

The CO saw our point of view and turned to the SWO.

"Get things moving immediately. If no-one else is available, get that bloody WAAF back from leave, I don't want a riot on my hands and this camp wrecked."

Soon after that, the 'Demob Machine' started up and processing began. We were given discharge papers, rail warrants, back pay, medical checks, clothes (the famous 'Demob Suit') and lorries ferried us to the railway station and finally, after seven years, I was a civilian again.

My first week as a civilian was spent in bed with Malaria, which had flared up again. When I recovered I went back to my old job as a boiler fireman at Bradshaw Bleach Works. But, like a lot of servicemen returning from the war, I could not settle. I went from job to job until I got a job lorry driving, which I settled down to for over twenty years.

In that time two more sons arrived and we were living in a local council house. As I was just settling down to family life I received a letter from the RAF offering me my rank of Sergeant, which I was seriously considering, but when I asked about married living quarters I was told that there was a two year waiting list.

I was not prepared to be separated again, I had been away from my family long enough, and in two years I could be posted overseas again, so I said thank you but no thank you.

❖ ❖ ❖

~ Chapter 7 ~

The Territorial Army ~ 1949-1970

I later received another letter from the RAF, but this one didn't give me the choice but told me to report for VR training at Bow Lee in Manchester. It was about this time that the Korean War was starting (amongst other skirmishes, e.g. Malaya, etc). Due to the nature of my trade as a Signaller, and my service record, I was still listed as a VR.

Not wanting to be sent to some far-flung British outpost again, I began to think how I could avoid this. Then I hit upon a brilliant idea, or I thought it was. I went to the Territorial Army Depot in Bolton where the Artillery Regiment did their training and administration.

I reported to the Adjutant, who was an ex-Jap POW. I told him my plight and asked if the TA could use my skills. He asked me what I did in the RAF and I told him I was a Wireless Operator/Signaller.

He asked me if I could drive, which was a silly question, as I had told him I was a transport driver, but he had to ask, I assured him I could. He then took me to the wireless stores and pointing to a wireless set asked me if I could set that up. I thought he was joking. It was a 19 set, to me more like a toy. He gave me a frequency and in less than a minute I had set it up.

"You are just the man we want", he said.

"Great, Thank you very much Sir," I replied.

"There is just one thing, I am ex RAF and know nothing about Artillery work."

"Oh, don't worry about that, just come down on drill nights and we will sort out the rest."

They did. A week or two later I got a letter from the RAF.

'HONOURABLE DISCHARGE: Reason for Discharge. RE-ENLISTMENT in ROYAL ARTILLERY, TERRITORIAL ARMY.'

So began twelve years of being a weekend soldier, and I enjoyed every minute of it. Due to my lack of experience in the TA I was enlisted as a corporal, but I had only been in a few weeks and I was offered my third stripe.

But at that time a lot of National Service lads had joined and some were very good Artillery soldiers, so I said that I would never ask one of my squad to do something I couldn't do myself, and better, so I refused my third stripe until I satisfied myself that I could gain their respect. Two years later I accepted my third stripe.

In my duties as Battery Signals Sergeant I instructed signals, radio, line laying and operating. I was also one of the driving instructors.

I had been in the Regiment a few months when Armistice Remembrance Sunday came round, and orders for the parade were given out. One sentence gave me a bit of a problem. I had been sporting my campaign ribbons on my uniform but I had not received the actual medals, and the orders were, 'Medals will be worn!'

I had two friends at that time, one an ex-Chindit and the other an ex-naval submariner, and between them managed to rustle up their appropriate medals and advised me what I should do.

I wrote to Records and told them I was not in receipt of my medals and in due time I received the medals I had applied for, plus one more, the Victory medal. So that made five.

The TA social side was very good, including all ranks social nights, officer and senior ranks social nights. Of course even the best laid plans sometimes didn't go quite to plan during these social evenings and once or twice we had the usual gate crashers.

Shortly after one such episode we decided on a senior ranks/officers night and to avoid any gate crashers we decided the only entrance would be through the front which was a fairly narrow passage.

I assigned two young gunners to help out on the door, one to see to the cloakroom and one to check the invitation cards. The one I had chosen to check the cards was a big strong lad who did a bit of all-in wrestling.

I briefed the lad on the cloakroom first. I put a two shilling piece on a saucer and said, "Now, when anyone comes in and puts something in the saucer, take it out leaving the two bob there. Divide what you get between you two."

I said to the lad checking cards, "Now remember, no one, no matter who they are, or what they say, is to come in without an invitation card."

With that, I went to join Joan in the bar and enjoy the night.

A bit later the RSM came to me and said, "I think you had better go to the door and sort out your guard, there could be trouble."

I rushed down to the door, and there was my 'guard' on the door, doing just what I had told him to do, but the person he was refusing entry to was the guest of honour, the Colonel of the Regiment!

I told the lad it was O.K. to let him in and apologised to the Colonel. I told him it was my fault as I had instructed the lad to not let anyone in if they had no card, no matter who they were. The Colonel laughed, and said, 'He certainly obeyed your orders. I asked him if he knew who I was and he said, 'Yes Sir, you are the Colonel, but Sergeant Shipperbottom said I was not to let anyone in, no matter who they were, without a card.'

I was pleased to see they can obey orders!

The Colonel and his wife joined us at our table, and frequently did so on future occasions, in fact his wife always joined Joan for a good chat. He would walk round, greeting everyone, and when he had finished his social duties he would join us saying, "Ah, how's our favourite sSergeant?"

Usually I would ask his wife to dance and he would dance with Joan., he had a great sense of humour, which displayed itself when I dropped a clanger.

On one of these events the Colonel went through his usual routine, and joined us, I asked his wife for a dance but the lady seemed to dance better and seemed more lively than usual. A little later, after the evening had mellowed everybody I said quietly to the Colonel, "Your good lady seems to be in good form tonight Sir."

He leaned over quietly to me, and whispered, "She's not my wife.'

I have dropped many 'clangers' in my service life but this was very embarrassing, I could not understand how I could have made such a mistake, I had not had a lot to drink, the room was well lit, and the Colonel was talking to another officer by this time so I tactfully let it pass.

On the next event the Colonel and his wife went through the usual routine and joined Joan and myself, then the Colonel broke the usual routine, he leaned over to me and said quietly, "Ask my wife to dance".

I did as requested and while we were dancing she said, "Oh thank you very much for the lovely compliment."

Not wishing to drop another clanger, I asked her, "I'm sorry, what do you mean?"

She laughed ,and said, "At the last dance you mistook my sister for me. I thought that was lovely compliment as she is twelve years younger than me!"

Being a smoothie, I replied, "No disrespect to your sister, but I would have said you were twins." The Shipperbottom stock went up a lot after that!

One of the gunners I was friendly with was, what I called, an 'accidental comedian' he was always making people laugh. He was going out with a very nice girl and one day he said that he and his girl were visiting someone near where I lived and he asked me what pub I went in.

I told him and he arranged to meet me. He turned up with his girl and when I went to buy a drink he told me that his girl didn't drink alcohol and asked me what kind of drink would I recommend. I said I would get her a suitable drink.

In all innocence I bought her a Cherry B, I thought it was a soft drink. She liked the drink and in the course of the night had quite a few and became a bit drunk. He ordered a taxi, he did have to help her into the taxi, and off they went.

A few weeks later he told me he was getting married and I congratulated him, and then he said,

"You and your bloody Cherry Bs did that. She's pregnant!"

He later passed his PSV and was working for the local bus company in Bolton. He did well on a couple of routes, and then he was put on the Affetside route.

After the signed bus stop at Bradshaw and Harwood there were no more fixed request stops as the area was rural, and passengers 'flagged' the bus to stop wherever they happened to be.

Unfortunately, nobody had told him and after he had made two trips without picking up a passenger after Harwood someone must have complained and an inspector was despatched to put him wise. When he told me about this, I found it very funny, especially when he said, "How was I to know? I thought the natives was just being friendly when they kept waving at me!"

The TA as a whole was a very hard working but happy regiment. I found being a signals instructor quite easy. Unlike the other instructors I didn't stand in front of the class and read the lecture from a book or written notes, I would tell the class what I knew on the subject of the lesson, in my own way, followed by a question and answer session.

On one occasion I had to take a class of officers and warrant officers on the subject of 'voice procedure' and I knew that two of the warrant officers from other batteries would be very keen to see me make a mistake and pick up on it. After all, they had been gunners for years and I was just a jumped-up RAF bloke trying to tell them how to do their job. I had been warned about this by my own Battery Sergeant Major. So I stood in front of them and they were all chatting away, not taking any notice of me, so I bellowed,

"GENTLEMEN! If I may say so, do you think you could behave with a little decorum!"

They went silent, so I continued in a quiet voice, "Now gentlemen, the subject this evening is voice procedure. Those of you who think you know it all and have nothing to learn can leave now. The others please listen and when I have finished we will have a question and answer session."

No one left, and when it was over my Battery Commander shook my hand and said,

"That was the best lecture they had ever attended on voice procedure. Well done sergeant!"

TA sessions were Sundays and one evening a week, usually Thursdays, work permitting, because with my job as a transport driver I spent many nights away from home during the week. We also had occasional weekend camps and every late spring, usually in early May, the Regiment went on a summer camp for two weeks, usually in the Brecon Beacons, South Wales.

At one of these camps we had been night shooting for four consecutive nights, using the 25-pounder field guns. The area was very difficult for signals, even in daylight, but when night fell it could become a nightmare. On this particular occasion it was a Regimental shoot and the Regimental command vehicle, the Battery command vehicles, and the Observation Post officers, all took up their various positions. Signals, known as a wireless 'Net', had been established between all command vehicles, both Regimental and Battery.

Once this had been set up, communication with the Observation Posts was tried. That is when problems arose. The wireless operator in our battery command post told me he could not raise the Observation Post. I tried without success.

So I tried out a theory I had studied years before, namely a ground aerial. I got out of my own vehicle, then went into the Command Post and studied the map to get our relative position to the Observation Post. Having acquired that knowledge, if my theory was correct, if I connected the ground aerial to the set, ran out the aerial wire in an arc of 180 degrees, reciprocal to the direction of the command post to the Observation Post, there should be a feedback to the set.

So I got two lads, one to inform me when the operator on the set got a signal and one to walk round with me to carry the counterpoises attached to the ground aerial. It worked a treat, we got a signal, I positioned the counterpoises in the ground at approximately 45 degrees to each other, and we were in business. A good strong signal to and from the Observation Post. Our command post was the only one in contact with the Observation Post, so all signals, fire orders, etc, were relayed through our Battery command post.

The same thing happened on the second night, so the signals officer from the Regimental command post asked me what I was doing. I told him I had laid out a ground aerial.

I told him to get a piece of aerial wire, connect it to the set, and walk in a circle with it. All that night, and the fourth night the Regimental Signals officer and signals Sergeant walked around the command post without success. The CO said that if ever they had to go to war, he wanted Sergeant Shipperbottom because, "Shipperbottom would smoke his bloody pipe and get signals through, come hell or high water."

One of the Observation Post officers was pleased too, because, coincidently, he was also an ex-RAF officer, so we had a lot in common. He later became my Battery Commander.

On another of these camps I marched with a German Panzer Regiment. On this particular camp the second week was 'Fire and Movement' (speed into action, fire, and then move to another area). It tested gunnery, driving in convoy and, sometimes, tempers.

After one such exercise, we put up our tents in a field just outside Monmouth. Dead tired, we got our heads down for a good night's kip. As the exercise had finished, the following day we only had to clean stow and pack up ready to go home the next day.

At about 0300 there was a hell of a noise. Bumping, banging, motor engines roaring, and then through the tent lines came five or six tanks, German tanks. We were not amused at being woken from our slumbers, so we thought about how to repay the call the Germans had paid us.

It was tradition in the Regiment on the last night of camp, to have a general drink, all ranks, and finish up the night, at midnight with a comic march through the camp, led by the Regimental band. The band was augmented by anyone, and everyone, who could find something to bang or make a noise in time with the band. The favourite was dustbin lids, the old metal ones.

So, at midnight the boozy gunners formed up behind the band and off we went. First of all we marched round our camp and then down the road to where the Germans were billeted in huts. By this time the noise had reached a good pitch and it did us good to see the lights coming on in the German occupied huts. At first they stood there in their night attire and looked at us in amazement. Then, most surprisingly, they joined us, and marched back to our lines with us, laughing and joking.

So for the next couple of hours or so we drank together. One of them explained that the reason they came through our lines was that they hadn't been told we were there, and they were in our tent lines before they realised or could be stopped.

Anyway, we all had a good laugh and they thought it a good idea for all ranks to have a good get together and a grand 'march' to finish the camp. They said that they would adopt the idea on their future exercises. I don't know if they did, but it amused me in later years to think of a German Tank Division drunk and marching, making a hell of a noise at midnight, amongst their NATO allies.

Perhaps the most important and memorable occasion in the TA was when the Queen reviewed all the contingents from all the Regiments of the TA in Hyde Park. I was one of the contingent representing the Bolton Artillery 253 Regiment. We stayed overnight in a drill hall in Balham and then the following morning it was 'Bags of Bull' and Best Blues, etc.

Eventually we were lined up like a lot of toy soldiers, in neat straight lines, under the control of a number of Guards drill sergeants. Then, when they were finally satisfied with us, a Guards officer, nearer seven than six feet tall, took control and he had a voice to match his build. There were an estimated 3,000 TA and WAACs and everyone heard his every command. We had put on our greatcoats because it was rather cool and his first order was,

"Off greatcoats and put them on the ground behind you.' As if he could read our minds, he went on, "...and don't worry about them being stolen, they will be there when you come back." And they were.

The Guards officer then brought us all to attention and the Queen drove, or was driven, down the lines of us 'weekend soldiers'. She drove very slowly and, talking with others later, we all agreed that she seemed to make each one of us feel as if we were being personally inspected. Everyone seemed to agree with this.

Then came the order to march off, the WAACs first and then, line by line, on the orders of the Guards Officer, aided by his NCOs, we were despatched in columns of three.

When the WAACs moved off, the weather was nice and dry, but by the time it was our turn it was raining very hard, but that Guards Officer had so impressed us that not one of us attempted to pick up his greatcoat.

We were nearly at the end of the parade and by the time we got to the saluting base we were not only very wet but, after a thousand or two having passed by before us, the ground was a sea of mud, which made quite a mess of all our carefully prepared bull.

At the saluting base were the Royal Family and the Queen Mother gave us all a warm smile as if it was a summers day. I don't know what the Guards band was playing but I know that we were all whistling 'Colonel Bogey'.

Despite the rain it was still a day to remember and forever after when that parade is mentioned (generally among TA or ex-TA personnel), I say with pride, "I was on that Parade!"

All good things come to an end and, sad to relate, so did the TA Regiment. Most of the senior ranks time was coming to an end and the regiment was changed to an anti-aircraft battery.

The 25 pounders disappeared and were replaced by Bofors anti-aircraft guns, though what use they would be against modern fighter/bomber jets was beyond me, someone had thought long and hard at this one!

I was watching them come into the drill hall, when a young officer, who was to be in charge of the 'detachment', asked me what I thought of the guns, and if I liked them.

I told him that I had seen those guns in action during the war, and if they did manage to shoot an aircraft down it was because the pilot was tired of life and used that way to commit suicide.

The young officer wasn't pleased when I said that the 25-pounder field gun was more use. Along with myself there were a few of the senior ranks finishing anyway.

❖ ❖ ❖

~ CHAPTER 8 ~

And Finally ~ 1970-1990

I HAD LEFT THE REGIMENT QUITE a time when I got a letter from War Office. The letter just said, 'Compliments of the War Office' and accompanied a medal – The Territorial Efficiency Medal – solid silver with my number, rank and name inscribed around the edge.

I have seen many letters in the British Legion journal complaining of the class difference between ex-Territorial officers and other ranks. An ex-TA officer gets a TA medal and can put TD (Territorial Distinction) after his name but other ranks cannot put TEM after their names, although the medals are awarded for the same reasons.

I was not bothered about that myself. I know the Territorial Efficiency Medal is a recommended medal, so if someone thought I was worth it, I was satisfied with that.

So, after over thirty years attachment to the Armed Forces, I finished up with six medals and a host of memories, a few which I thought worth recording here for posterity.

To replace my activities with the TA I became an active member of the ROAB (Royal Order of Alluvium Buffaloes) and the British Legion. I became Pensions Officer for the Legion, sick visitor, secretary, stand-in Treasurer and Delegate to PGL for the Buffs. I have been to re-unions both of the ASR and the gunners, and most of the five COs I served under in the TA.

While living in Romford for a short time, Joan and I had a fairly good social life with the Buffs, Legion, and Royal Air Force Association. Life is a bit quieter now, but then at our age we need to quieten down a bit, though my wife does not agree wholly on that point.

After retirement we moved to Haslingden and I was asked to carry on the job of Pensions Officer for the Haslingden branch of the Legion, which I did for a number of years. When I said I was resigning, the Branch asked me to form a Service Committee with myself as Chairman, which I did for a number of years.

❖ ❖ ❖

Endnotes & References

1. The Pretoria Pit Disaster, 1910

This was the worst coal mining accident to have occurred in Lancashire and the third worst mining disaster in British history. The Pretoria Pit was a complex of coal mines owned by the Hulton Colliery Company and situated on the border of Westhoughton and Atherton. Pretoria Pit was the largest coal mine in the Westhoughton area, working five coal seams in the region. Each seam had its own mine: Trencherbone, Plodder, Yard, Three-Quarter and Arley mines. The Hulton Colliery Co. employed approximately 2,500 people locally. On the morning of 21st December 1910, a total of 898 men and boys clocked in for the day shift at the Hulton Colliery and most had descended the shafts below ground before 8:00am. At 7:50am there was a tremendous underground explosion, about 300 yards deep below the earth's surface, at the level of the Yard mine. The blast had been reportedly heard and felt up to four miles away, and initially claimed the lives of 343 of the 347 men working in the Yard mine that fateful morning. Some close to the source of the blast died instantly, others suffocated due to the ensuing high levels of trapped carbon dioxide and carbon monoxide gasses – or 'after-damp', as the miners called it. There were a few minor injuries reported from the neighbouring Trencherbone and Arley mines, although some working those seams were also sickened by the gas, but there were no fatalities at these other mines as they were separately ventilated via the No.4 shaft. All 343 men that perished that day were working in the Yard mine. One body was never recovered and six were registered as 'unknown'. It took weeks to bury the dead, funerals were even held on Christmas Day.

Source http://www.staveley-genealogy.com/pretoria_pit.htm

2. The Zeppelin Raid on Bolton, 1914

This event was recalled in the account below from *Bolton Evening News* 21st March 2014:

The German airship would have been a terrifying sight. It was almost 600 feet long and 60 feet in diameter. The bombs caused the most devastation to No 58 Kirk Street, where the Irwins lived, and their neighbours' homes at numbers 60, 62 and 64.

These were neighbours who, undoubtedly, chatted over their garden walls, borrowed cups of sugar from each other and helped out in times of crisis. This would be a crisis that would rip the heart out of their community.

The airship was commanded by Kurt Frankenburg who was, he says, an experienced German officer and had a crew of 17. The zeppelin carried a huge load of explosive and high incendiary bombs. The zeppelin was actually lost and it is thought Frankenburg believed he was flying over Derby. He had already dropped bombs over Holcombe, Rossendale and Ramsbottom, and a further two incendiaries over Greenmount in Bury that night.

He then drifted over Astley Bridge and Sharples, dropping a bomb that narrowly missed the Eden Orphanage. He then went on to Halliwell where windows were broken by explosives in Darley Street. The next bomb destroyed a terraced house in Lodge Vale, but the three women who lived there escaped with shock and minor injuries.

Incendiaries fell on Waldeck Street and Chorley Old Road. From there the airship passed over Queens Park, the River Croal and the railway lines. Another incendiary fell on Wellington Street, setting a house on fire and trapping a woman and two children in an upstairs bedroom. Thankfully, the fire brigade were able to save them.

At this point no-one had been badly hurt.

Frankenburg, possibly aiming at the Eagle Mill, then dropped the five bombs over Kirk and John Streets. These rows of terraced houses connected Deane Road and Derby Street at the point where the University of Bolton and College Way now stand. There six houses were destroyed and 13 people were killed.

3. The Gamekeeper's Cottage, The Jumbles

The Gamekeeper's Cottage was built in the late 1700s near the site of a Corn Mill, which was sited next to a water goit to provide power to mill the corn. The mill dated back to around 1542 and was positioned to give good access for the local farmers to bring their corn to be milled. The mill had an associated kiln to dry the corn which was powered by the coal from the Bradshaw Pits, which yielded a small amount of coal, just enough to supply the kiln.

When the Bleachworks was set up in the early 1800s the water powering the corn mill was required to feed the reservoirs for the Bleachworks further along the valley and in 1890 the corn mill was demolished.

The Gamekeeper's Cottage was then used by the Hardcastle family to house the Gamekeeper, whose job it was to ensure the continued flow of water to the reservoirs, along with normal Gamekeepr's duties.

Source: Thanks to James J. Francis (deceased) of the Turton History Society for the above information.

4. RAF Padgate

During the Second World War, Padgate had a small RAF Station. RAF Padgate will be well-remembered by thousands of young men who were selected for RAF National Service and on this site received their first taste of military discipline, ill-fitting uniforms and a severe haircut.

The site of the former RAF station was demolished in the late 1990s and since then the site has been largely covered by a Bellway housing estate, bordered by various other local amenities and suburbs of Warrington – Bennett's Rec (where the Cheshire Cadets Drum and Bugle Corps are based) and the railway line to the south, Fearnhead to the North-East,

Blackbrook and Cinnamon Brow to the northern side. University Academy Warrington (a secondary school, originally known as Padgate High School and then renamed as Lysander Community High School) is also sited on this land.

The main entrance to the RAF camp was situated on what is now called Station Road North (re-named from its original Station Road title).

Although the RAF site is now largely invisible, its legacy lives on in local place names and so on - Insall Road running east-west in parallel to the A574 is named after the one-time commanding officer of the site (Group Captain Insall), the local high school University Academy Warrington (originally named Padgate High School when it was opened in the late 1970s) was known from 2009 to 2013 as Lysander Community High School, the Westland Lysander being one of the aircraft linked to the former RAF base.

Remnants of the camp's presence can still be seen in some parts of the land for example the brickwork from the rifle range can still be seen close to the railway footbridge in the south-west corner of the former site.

Source: Wikipedia

5. The Dieppe Raid

The Dieppe Raid, also known as the Battle of Dieppe, Operation Rutter and, later, Operation Jubilee was a Second World War Allied attack on the German-occupied port of Dieppe on the northern coast of France. The attack took place on 19th August 1942.

The attack began at 5:00am and by 10:50am the Allied commanders had to call a retreat. Over 6,000 infantrymen, mostly Canadian, were supported by a Canadian Armoured regiment. They were also helped by a strong force of Royal Navy and smaller Royal Air Force group.

The goal was to capture a major port for a short period and to gather information. Upon retreat, the Allies also wanted to destroy coastal defences, port structures and important buildings. The raid was also intended to improve morale and demonstrate the commitment of the United Kingdom to attack a Western Front in Europe.

None of these goals was achieved. There was not enough Allied artillery support. The troops were trapped on the beach by obstacles and German gunfire. After less than 10 hours since the first landings, the last Allied troops had all been either killed, evacuated, or captured by the Germans.

Instead of showing the British commitment, the terrible number of Allied deaths showed that the Allies were not ready to invade France for a long time.

However, the attack did help the Allies to gather some information.

A total of 3,623 of the 6,086 men (almost 60%) who went ashore were either killed, wounded, or captured. The Royal Air Force did not get the Luftwaffe to start a battle. The RAF lost 96 aircraft (at least 32 to being shot down or accidents), compared to 48 lost by the Luftwaffe.

The Royal Navy lost 33 landing craft and one destroyer. The events at Dieppe affected the plans for the North African (Operation Torch) and Normandy landings (Operation Overlord).

Source Wikipedia

6. Wingate's Second Expedition

The Chindits were the largest of all the Allied Special Forces of World War II. Formed and led by Major-General Orde Wingate DSO, they fought behind enemy lines in Northern Burma during 1943 and 1944 in the war against Japan. They were unconventional due to their total reliance on airdrops for their supplies and complete dependence on wireless for communications.

In March 1942 Lieutenant Colonel Wingate arrived in India after carrying out successful guerrilla operations in Palestine and Abyssinia. Using his understanding of guerrilla warfare, he proposed a scheme of long-range penetration operations deep into enemy-held territories in Burma. In July 1942 the 77th Indian Infantry Brigade was formed for this task.

Wingate organised and specially trained the Chindits in commando methods, preparing them for jungle fighting, sabotage, and air supply dropping.

The Chindits infiltrated deep into Northern Burma and for many months they lived and fought in the jungle, hundreds of miles behind the Japanese forward positions.

Their mission was to disrupt the enemy's lines of communication, blowing bridges, railway tracks and blocking supply routes. They would harass the enemy to cause confusion, disrupt their plans and divert their resources.

The Chindits were organised into columns with a strength of about 340. Each column was strong enough to defend itself and capable of mounting surprise attacks on enemy targets, yet small enough for concealment and for mobility to evade and slip through enemy nets. Columns would combine to strike larger targets and then disappear back into the jungle.

There were two Chindit expeditions into Burma, the first in February 1943, code-named ***Operation Longcloth***, consisted of a force of 3,000 men who marched over 1,000 miles during the campaign. It was an experimental operation to prove British forces could operate many hundreds of miles from their own bases in the midst of Japanese controlled territory and to test Wingate's theories and to gain experience.

The second expedition, in March 1944, was on a much larger scale and consisted of a force of 20,000 men. They were given the name ***Special Force*** and was composed mainly of British battalions supplemented by Burma Rifles, Gurkha and Nigerian battalions and a company of Hong Kong volunteers.

Wingate had wanted an airborne invasion, to assist this United States provided an air task force to be known as 1st Air Commando. Equipped with bomber, fighter, transport, glider and light aircraft they provided the Chindits with direct air support and evacuated their casualties. The fly-in of the bulk of the force, codenamed ***Operation Thursday***, was by the RAF and 1st Air Commando. Gliders were used to land advance parties who then constructed airstrips for the transport planes. It was the second-largest airborne invasion of World War II.

Once inside Burma, well-defended strongholds were established from which columns operated, air supply drop zones were established and nearby airstrips were built for evacuating casualties. Floater columns patrolled outside the perimeter of the stronghold to counter-attack the flanks and rear of any enemies approaching or attacking the stronghold.

Tragically, their leader, General Wingate, was killed in a plane crash a few weeks after the launch of Operation Thursday. Towards the end of their operations, the Chindits came under new command and their plans were changed. They were used for tasks that they were not trained for or equipped for and were kept in the field much longer than Wingate had planned. Casualties were high.

7. The Ramree Island Massacre

World War II was nearing its end. The Japanese Imperial Army had invaded Ramree Island in Burma located off the Bay of Bengal in 1942. In 1945 the Allied Forces unlocked the Burma Mission with the purpose of pushing the Japs out of Burma. Joint forces of 36th Indian Infantry Brigade and units of British Royal Marine were dispatched on 26th January 1945 for Ramree with two tasks: (1) push the Japs out and (2) build an airbase.

The Allied forces arrived but met with fierce resistance from the Japanese. What followed was a bloodbath by artillery and gunfire. However, the worst was yet to come. After a heavy battle, the Allied force managed to flank the Japanese from all sides and nearly 1,000 Japanese soldiers were trapped. The Allied troops repeatedly offered the Japanese soldiers the opportunity to surrender and lay down their weapons.

Unfortunately, the Japanese, who thought of surrender as worse than death, started looking for escape routes. The only route they could see was a tidal swampland sweeping over an area of 16 kilometres. The swampland was dense and definitely not friendly. However, the Japs decided to cross it, hoping to merge with a larger Japanese force stationed on the other side.

In beeline formation, the Japanese soldiers started crossing the swampland. Beneath the underbrush was sticky mud in which slithered scorpions, snakes and poisonous spiders. Adding to the misery were mosquito swarms. Still determined to cross instead of surrendering, the Japanese soldiers continued but in the process, many started to succumb to the diseases brought by the mosquitoes. For several days they continued, despite having no drinking water or food. In the meantime, the Allied forces positioned on the banks of the swamp were firing artillery shells to make things even more difficult for them.

As if snakes, scorpions, spiders, mosquitoes and Allied shellfire were not enough, the Japanese now met with something even more dreadful. One night an Allied patrol heard frantic screams along with gunshots in the darkness of the night.

The Japanese were unaware that the swamp they were trying to cross was infested with saltwater crocodiles that could grow to 20 feet or more.

What followed was the bloodiest massacre of World War II not caused by humans.

Of the 1,000 Japanese soldiers, only about 20 managed to survive and later reported that the crocs had simply appeared from nowhere and attacked from all sides.

Although it is unclear exactly how many of the Japanese were killed by crocodiles as opposed to the other elements of their ordeal, the Ramree Island crocodile massacre earned a place in the *Guinness Book of World Records* for being the maximum number of human deaths caused by a single attack by crocodiles.

Source: https://factslegend.org/the-ramree-island-crocodile-massacre-a-horrific-carnage/

8. RMS Mooltan

RMS Mooltan was an ocean liner and Royal Mail Ship of the Peninsular and Oriental Steam Navigation Company (P&O). She was ordered in 1918 and completed in 1923. She served in the Second World War first as the armed merchant cruiser HMS *Mooltan* (F75) and then as a troop ship. She was retired from P&O service in 1953 and scrapped in 1954.

Source: Wikipedia

9. Durban's Lady in White

Perla Siedle Gibson was a South African soprano and artist who became internationally celebrated during the Second World War as the Lady in White, when she sang troopships in and out of Durban harbour.

Gibson was born in Durban in 1888, the daughter of Otto Siedle, a prominent local shipping agent, businessman and musician of German extraction. In the early twentieth century she studied music and art in Europe and the US, and gave recitals in London and New York. Her youngest brother was Jack Siedle, the South African Test cricketer.

During World War 2 Durban was an extremely busy waystation for convoys of ships en route to the fronts in North Africa and the Far East. Gibson became famous among thousands of Allied troops when she serenaded them as their ships passed in and out.

One account of the origin for Gibson's custom was that it arose when she was seeing off a young Irish seaman her family had entertained the day before. As his ship was departing he was said to have called across the water asking her to sing something Irish, and Gibson responded with a rendition of "When Irish Eyes are Smiling". She decided to sing to every ship connected with the war which entered or left the harbour. Over the following years she went on to sing to more than 5,000 ships and a total of about a quarter of a million Allied servicemen. Clad in white with a red hat, she would stand at a spot at the mouth of Durban Bay where ships entering and leaving the harbour pass quite close, and sing patriotic and sentimental songs through a megaphone from a torpedoed ship, which grateful British soldiers had given her.

Soldiers' talk led to the fame of the Lady in White spreading around the world. A British army newspaper called *Parade*, dated 3rd March 1945, described Gibson as a highlight of troops' visits to Durban:

'As the crowded ships passed into the harbour, men lining the landward rails saw a woman, dressed in white, singing powerfully through a megaphone such songs as "There'll Always be an England!" and "Land of Hope and Glory." A well-known local figure, she would drive down from her home on the Berea as soon as she could see that the ships were moving in.'

Gibson was married to Air Sergeant Jack Gibson, who served in Italy, and had two sons and a daughter in the military. She had sung all their ships goodbye as they left for the war. She even sang on the day she received news that her son Roy had been killed in the fighting in Italy.

She died in 1971, shortly before her 83rd birthday. The year later a bronze plaque donated by men of the Royal Navy was erected to her memory on Durban's North Pier on the spot where she used to sing. In 1995 Queen Elizabeth II unveiled a statue of Gibson near the Ocean Terminal in Durban harbour.

The statue of Perla Gibson was re-located to the Port Natal/Durban Maritime Museum on 27th September 2016.

(*Source*: Wikipedia)